LEANN AL

SCREAMING
ON THE INSIDE

A JOURNEY TO FREEDOM

Leann Albrecht

ACCLAIM FOR *Screaming on the Inside*

"It is one thing to read a book by someone you do not know and yet who has suffered for the beauty on the page. It is quite another to watch a friend hurt and weep and reach for God in heartache and then to read in astonishment the inner glory wrung from her life. This is how I feel about Leann Albrecht's writing. I have been her pastor, her friend, her co-laborer. She is an authentic woman of God. Yet who knew that she could capture that authenticity so tenderly on the page and summon us all to greater depth and greater spiritual passion."

—STEPHEN MANSFIELD, New York Times Bestselling Author

"I have watched Leann Albrecht lead thousands in worship and this book will lead thousands into new vistas of healing and forgiveness. Thank you, Leann, for your candid and magnificent work, written from the heart as only you can do!"

—DR. JOHN STANKO, Pastor, Allegheny Alliance Church, Pittsburgh, PA

"Leann's words touched me deeply. She has been one of my favorite worship leaders for years; I had no idea she was 'screaming on the inside.' Like me, I know you will be profoundly encouraged by this book."

—MARILYN MEBERG, Speaker and Writer for Women of Faith

"In this very raw, real, and brave book, Leann pulls out all the stops to show the reasons we all scream on the inside. By the end of the book, you will know the God Whom Leann worships."

—PATSY CLAIRMONT, Author of *Kaleidoscope* and Speaker for Women of Faith

Contact Information:
Leann Albrecht
High Hill Songs
P.O. Box 1533
Goodlettsville, TN 37072 USA
615-851-2850
www.leannalbrecht.com
lmalbrect@aol.com
Facebook—Leann Albrecht Fan Club

Author note: Some of the names of the people mentioned in this book have been changed when I felt anonymity was essential.

ISBN: 978-0-9830214-2-1

Printed the United States of America.

Dedication

Carl, my wonderful husband, has been a constant source of encouragement in writing this book. He gave me the courage to keep breathing, find one more word, and complete one more paragraph. I had no idea what a daunting task and emotional expenditure it would be to bare my soul in these pages. But Carl's love lifted me to share the secrets of my heart as a path to freedom for others.

So, I dedicate this book to Carl. Thank you, love of my life.

Contents

Acknowledgements

MY MOM AND DAD'S PIONEERING SPIRIT shaped my passion for life. I don't ever remember Jack Hendrickson being afraid. Even when he taunted catastrophe, he always came through it unscathed. It seemed that God assigned extra angels to take care of him.

Part of his fearlessness may have come from growing up on an island in the Mississippi River. Crossing two rivers every day in an open skiff made him keenly aware of how to live with, and against, nature. Many times they would have lost their lives had God not intervened. He wrote of these adventures in his book, "True Tales From Mark Twain Land." (www.truetalesbook.com)

My niece, Allison Hendrickson, laughingly said one day, "You Hendrickson's always live on the edge of pending disaster, but I always know everything will turn out OK. God always takes care of you guys."

Dad and mom's courage taught me to be strong and never give up—even in the face of hopeless odds. The pillars of their faith rested firmly on a history of God's faithfulness.

My mother, Mary, nursed my bumps and scrapes. She taught me how to cook, organize, and make every dwelling into a home. My appreciation for critters and all living things came through our frequent walks together, admiring God's great handiwork. She taught me to work and finish a project and she taught me to pray. Time after time, I saw God answer her prayers. Through her deep love, simplicity of faith, and compassion, I came to understand the gentle side of God.

Carl has been my constant companion and best friend during our twenty-six years of marriage. He believed in me even when I didn't believe in myself. He has always been my biggest cheerleader. Other than Jesus, he is the greatest stabilizer in my life. Thank you, Carl, for embracing life with me.

When the Lord told me to write this book, I wondered if I heard Him right. I had never even written a poem or article. When I talked about it with Stephen Mansfield, who was our pastor at the time, he said he would help me. And he did. I am grateful and humbled to have been coached by one of the greatest wordsmiths of our time. Thank you, Stephen for sharing your wealth of writing wisdom with me. I am forever grateful that you kept nudging me to the finish line.

My dear friend, Linda Forrest, has gone far beyond the call of duty in helping me edit this book. I tend to read what I want to say rather than reading what I wrote. So, to help me hear what I actually wrote, Linda tirelessly read the stories back to me. We laughed and we cried together through that process. Thank you Linda for your friendship, and for your hours of love, prayer and dedication for this project.

Dr. Diana Corzo, I will never forget your generous labor of love in your many hours of editing as a psychologist. Thank you for your professional perspective.

I also thank you, Meng Yeen and Poh Wah Lee. Your love, prayers and support made this book possible. I am deeply grateful for your help in turning this project into a reality.

To all my family, friends and intercessors who have been praying for this book to be released. I felt your prayers as I wrote. Thank you.

Most of all, thank you Lord for carrying me through the journey of life. Your love is amazing!!

Introduction

THERE IS NOT A MAN, WOMAN OR CHILD who does not experience the pain of growing up. Disappointments and suffering are a part of everyone's life. Many times we internalize our grief because it is embarrassing, overwhelming, or we simply don't know how to deal with it. We consciously or subconsciously resolve to bury it so we are the only one who can hear our screams of torment. We long to crawl out of the hole of hopelessness and live in a land of light and peace, but we haven't found the key to unlock the door to our inner solitary confinement.

As we go about our lives at home and at work we might look like we have everything together. In fact, we become quite skilled at covering up and camouflaging our internal struggles. No one would ever know the isolation that accompanies the ache in our soul.

I know this because I have lived it. I was one who suffered in silence. I didn't know who could help me, or more importantly, whom I could trust. There were no easy answers so I simply stuffed it.

I tried to mask my condition with activities, hoping to outrun the pain. I thought, "If I just busy myself, it will distract me and I won't feel it anymore." I tried medicating with alcohol to drown the pain but only drowned my liver and woke up with a headache. There was no "time-release" medication that worked 24 hours a day. Inevitably, when I closed the door behind me at night, I could still hear my desperate cries for help resounding through the hallways of my heart. They were my constant companions. I hadn't outsmarted them and they hadn't gone away, I had only temporarily muffled their sounds.

Jesus said we would encounter trouble in life. He promised He would never leave us but would carry us through every difficulty.

He desires that we be free from the pain of our past, whether it's physical, mental, emotional or spiritual.

The first step to freedom is to stop running, turn around and face the pain. In the next eleven chapters, you'll read true stories that hold the keys to becoming pain free. They are raw, gutsy and real. I invite you to journey with me while I go from pain to peace. Permit the Lord to empower your faith and bring complete healing to your body, mind and spirit. Don't be afraid. The Lord is with you and is waiting to help you like He patiently waited to help me.

I can write about my experiences now because there is no more pain attached to the events and sufferings of my past. Even though they were some of the hardest times of my life, it was through them I discovered His unconditional love and won my greatest victories of faith. I have allowed the Lord to heal those wounds and He has quieted my soul within me. I no longer scream on the inside.

Chapter 1
FRIENDSHIP WITH GOD

IN 1960, MY DAD PASTORED A LITTLE COUNTRY CHURCH in Mosier, Illinois. The old wooden frame building—where we met every Sunday morning, Sunday night, and Wednesday night—was not a comfortable, or comforting—place. It had no carpeting or padded pews. The eerie creaks of the hardwood floors made me feel hollow and cold inside. Our family was always the first to arrive. We had a routine—things like straightening and sweeping the welcome mat, clearing cobwebs, turning on lights, building a fire in cold weather, etc. I was always relieved when people started arriving. Their smiling faces brought life and softened the harshness of the old Christian Church.

I liked to sing along with mom and dad as they led the song service. I held a hymnal and pretended to read the words. Dad was so handsome; I loved to watch him preach even though I didn't understand much of what he said unless he told a Bible story. He was a great storyteller.

Longwinded guest speakers were downright agonizing for me. It seemed like hours crept by as they preached and I fidgeted. Mom frequently "shushed" me because every time I squirmed, the rickety pew would squeak. I just couldn't get comfortable and didn't understand how a human being was supposed to sit on those hard straight-back wooden benches. I had never seen anyone with a square bottom.

You wouldn't think a three-year-old squirming little girl would retain very much from church. But apparently I did. One morning, sitting alone in our living room, I looked out at the carpet of green grass that blanketed the hillside behind our country home. Such a peaceful spot, it was my favorite place to gaze out of the window.

As I quietly sat there, an unusual feeling came over me. I felt homesick, even though I was right there at home. I felt like I did when I missed mom or dad. But mom was in the kitchen, cleaning up breakfast dishes, and dad always came home for lunch. Who was I longing for? Right then, I realized I had a deep desire to be with Jesus. It felt like we had been apart for a long time; I missed Him terribly. But that didn't make sense to me. Even though I had heard Bible stories about Him, I had never personally met Him. How could I be longing for Him?

 Earlier that morning, I had asked Mom to play my favorite slate record on the wind-up Victrola. In fact, I liked it so much I asked her to play it nearly every day. The gospel choir, singing "Beyond the Sunset," captivated me once again. Even though I didn't know the meaning of all the words, that song carried me away.

Beyond the sunset, O blissful morning
When with our Savior, Heav'n is begun
Earth's toiling ended, O glorious dawning
Beyond the sunset when day is done

Beyond the sunset no clouds will gather
No storms will threaten, no fears annoy
O day of gladness, O day unending
Beyond the sunset, eternal joy

Beyond the sunset, O glad reunion
With our dear loved ones who've gone before
In that fair homeland, we'll know no parting
Beyond the sunset, forevermore. [2]

 As I listened to those words over and over again, I wanted to know that Person, the One who lived "beyond the sunset." I longed for Him; I wanted Him to be my friend. So in my simple childish way I said, "Jesus, I don't want you to live so far away. Would you come and live with me?" As I prayed those words, tears ran down my face. Instantly, I felt Jesus make my heart His home. I could feel Him wrap His arms around me. The warmth of

His love reached all the way to my deepest parts. I felt happy from the inside out. In fact, I didn't want the moment to end, so I stayed there with Him for what seemed a long, long time.

When I finally got up from the couch, Jesus got up with me. No matter where I went, He was there. The heaven that was "beyond the sunset" came to me that day and filled me with His light and love. My three-year-old mind didn't fully comprehend what had just happened, but that day was the beginning of my friendship with God.

Over the summer, I learned to swim and dad started teaching my brother, Mark, and me to sing. At first, we sang the melody with him. Then he started teaching us how to sing harmony. Dad would sing a note, and then tell me to stay on that note. He found another note in the chord for Mark and told him to sing that one. But as soon as I heard Mark's new note, I couldn't hear mine any-more, so I wandered to his note. That tickled us and we had to start the process all over again. After a while, Dad wouldn't think it was funny anymore and we got into trouble because we couldn't stop laughing. Finally, Dad hung a towel between Mark and me to keep us from looking at each other and giggling. It worked. Eventually, we were able to pick out our own harmonies and sang along in three-parts.

In 1963, when we moved to Versailles, Illinois, I was so glad my new friend, Jesus, went with me as I started first grade. I didn't adjust well to school. Although I received good grades, I never seemed to fit in with the other kids. The little girls had their cliques and made it clear that I wasn't cool enough to be one of them. I cried in the bathroom because they treated me so badly. It was always such a relief when the last class bell rang so I could race to our home four blocks away. I didn't stop running until I crashed though the front door. When the screen door banged behind me, I felt safe again. I was home.

Special privileges came with being the preacher's kid. Dad was a pastor, but he was also a pioneer. He always pushed us past the

boundaries of piety. One day, he committed the "irreverent" act of giving us permission to swim in the church baptistery. So, one Sunday
night, after everyone else had gone home, we turned out the lights. A
damp musty fragrance rose from the tank as we quietly lifted the old
hinged wooden door. Just before we jumped in, Dad told us, "Now,
you have to keep this a secret." We all knew the elders would frown
on such impious activity. With a quick promise, we plunged in. I
thought, "This must be what it feels like to be rich. We have our very
own pool in the floor of the church sanctuary. Life is good!"

Soon, we moved to Pontoosuc, Illinois, a small town on the Mississippi River, where Dad was pastor of a non-denominational church.
Every Sunday morning, he let Mark and me ring the bell from the
belfry in the vestibule. I couldn't wait to hear its loud bong reverber-
ate through the neighborhood, letting everyone know church was
about to start. Dad unhooked the long rope that was safely hung
near the ceiling. Then the three of us pulled it down hard causing
the huge cast iron bell to clang. Mark and I took turns clinging to
the rope as the weight of the bell pulled us all the way to the ceiling… squealing with delight. After six or seven rings, Dad would
say, "That's enough, kids. It's time to start church now." Reluctantly,
we handed the rope back to him and made our way to the second
row pew.

Other than ringing the bell, Sunday School was my favorite part
of church. I especially liked it when mom taught the class. I liked
her gentle and comforting voice. She often used a flannel board
as her visual aide when telling Bible stories. Each animal or character was hand-cut from velvet, which would stick to the flannel.
She often asked me to help her place the cutout characters on the
board at the right time in the story. It was such a great feeling to be
needed as I caressed the velvet figures, waiting for the next scene.

Growing up, I tried to do the right thing—like reading my
Bible every day and singing in church when my parents asked.
We were always involved in ministry…either traveling or at our
home church. I enjoyed my friends at church but going to school

remained a difficult thing. Not having buddies in class didn't get easier; I just learned to live with it. Instead of laughing and talking with other kids in the halls, I was usually alone. However, I took comfort in knowing my true Friend was always with me.

I was "born again" as a child, baptized with water at twelve, and then baptized in the Spirit and received my heavenly language when I was thirteen. Even though these spiritual experiences were authentic moments; my relationship with Jesus remained juvenile. I was like a child who learned the alphabet but never learned to speak the language.

Even when I entered the tumultuous and hormone-raging teen years, the divine encounter on the couch, at three years old, remained my anchor point. I never forgot He lived inside of me. Even when I rebelled, I knew He was still with me. In whatever I did, I knew when I turned around, He would be there waiting for me.

During those years, I became completely self-centered. Basically, I called on Him when I got in trouble and He would somehow bail me out. I had very little passion to get to know Him or deepen our relationship.

The moments of tenderness with the Lord that I knew as a child seemed distant. That left me wondering, *what was real and what was just childhood emotions.* There were times when it felt like I was simply going through the motions of what I was being taught in church.

I think the Lord knew it was time for me to grow up. *"The Lord disciplines those he loves, as a father the son he delights in."* — PROVERBS 3:12. Like a master trainer taking a dog for a walk, there comes a time when the master trains the dog to walk beside him instead of in front of him, always pulling on the leash. My day of training had arrived.

That training lasted several years. Much of the story will be told in later chapters. But, I want to tell you one of those stories now. In 1992, my husband Carl and I moved to Nashville. My calendar was full of recording sessions, conferences and tour dates as a back-up singer with several artists. I was flying high through life. Work and friends were plentiful and everything seemed to be going my way. I was very proud of myself for being good at what I did. I felt smug about "hanging out" with famous people and about climbing the social ladder.

Then the same Jesus, who met me as a child, allowed everything in my life to collapse. Within days, most of my scheduled "gigs" cancelled! Some of the cancellations had legitimate reasons while others had no explanation. I was left completely bewildered. The bubble of favor around me popped. Even after many attempts to get work, I couldn't land a single job. No one seemed to need a singer…or at least they didn't need me.

In desperation, I cried out to the Lord like I had always done before. This time, He was silent. It didn't matter how pitifully I pleaded, I could get no response from Him. As the weeks went by, I felt tormented by His silence and by my lack of work. Anxiety began to build. Fear of the future became a tsunami. I knew something was terribly wrong but I didn't know what I had done. I even wondered if I had unknowingly committed the unpardonable sin because He wasn't speaking to me and I couldn't sense His nearness. He felt so far away.

Then one day, in my desperation, I was reading the Bible when these words seemed to be illuminated on the page:

> *"But then I will win her back once again. I will lead her into the desert and speak tenderly to her there. I will return her vineyards to her and transform the Valley of Trouble into a gateway of hope. She will give herself to me there, as she did long ago when she was young, when I freed her from her captivity in Egypt. When that day comes," says the Lord, "you will call me 'my husband' instead of 'my master.' O Israel, I will wipe the many names of Baal from your lips, and you will never mention*

them again. On that day I will make a covenant with all the wild animals and the birds of the sky and the animals that scurry along the ground so they will not harm you. I will remove all weapons of war from the land, all swords and bows, so you can live unafraid, in peace and safety. I will make you my wife forever, showing you righteousness and justice, unfailing love and compassion. I will be faithful to you and make you mine, and you will finally know me as the Lord. —Hosea 2:14-20[3]

Suddenly, His silence was over. He *spoke to me!* Beyond this Word from Hosea that came alive, He said to me, "This is what I am doing with you right now. I am stripping everything away from your life so that all you have left is Me. I want you to *know* Me, not only for what I can do for you, but for WHO I AM."

I was so relieved to hear His voice again. As I wept, my eyes were opened to the fact that He wanted my complete devotion and love for Himself. He wanted my undivided attention. My heart was very unbridled; I had been blinded by my selfishness.

He had pursued me when I was a little girl. Now, I suddenly realized I had never really pursued knowing Him. I had simply "used" the Lord for favors and sought Him for what He could do for me. He had become my "genie in a bottle." How could I have been so self-indulgent? I cried out for mercy. Through much weeping and sorrow, I told Him how sorry I was. In my brokenness, I found Him again.

The Lord had used silence to get my attention and now that He had it, I wanted to know where He was taking me. I wanted to know what this dry place—this desert or wilderness—was all about? As I began to search, I found that it's a place free of distractions, a dry barren uncultivated region with no inhabitants. Up to that point, my life had been full of activities. Now, everything was quiet and dry. This was going to be a huge adjustment! I wasn't sure how I was going to handle it. I had no reference for that kind of lifestyle. Even though I was a little afraid to get to know Him, I felt it would be OK because he said, *"I will be faithful to you and make you mine, and you will finally know me as the Lord."* —HOSEA **2:20**[4]

My life wasn't going to be about *me* anymore. It was going to be about *Him!* He had called me to a destiny that would never be fulfilled if I remained the most important part in my life. In His great love, it was my time to go through the school of discipline in order to make the transfer from my world of importance to His.

Through His training and discipline, He built my character and deepened my love and trust in Him. The hardest lesson was to "wait on Him." That required patience, and I had very little of it. He made me stop my incessant activities and sit still. As I obeyed, I began to use spiritual muscles that had never been exercised before.

My hunger to know Him grew. That year, all I wanted for my birthday was a study Bible. I devoured the pages using the cross-references, concordance and footnotes. God's Word became alive to me! As I studied it and listened to the Lord, He revealed His flawless character, and His kindness drew me closer. He lovingly touched the immaturity in my life. So I would read, cry, repent… read, cry and repent some more. As I wiped away the salty tears that stung my lips, I realized that transformation was finally taking place.

That season took about a year. Because most of my work was can-celled, our household income was dramatically reduced. However, the Lord always met our needs. Just when I thought we couldn't financially survive another day, He provided a small job that sustained us. Even in the testing and training, He was proving Himself faithful.

At the end of that season, I was in love with Jesus! He meant more to me than anything else in the world. I was conscious of every little thing I said and did because I didn't want to change our tender relationship. I was so glad He loved me enough to take me away to the "desert" so I could get to really know Him…to know His presence, His voice, and His love. He was always *my* true Friend. But after that season, I became *His* friend…a true friend of God.

APPLICATION STUDY GUIDE

Week One   [Date: _____]

Pick one day out of your week when you can take time to sit and reflect on the following thoughts and respond to the meditation questions below.

First Key To Becoming Free: *Become a Friend of God.*

Friendship means different things to different people. But, in simple terms, it is a close personal relationship of mutual affection and trust with another person. I see clear distinct stages of friendship:

- The first stage is when the purpose of a relationship is to "use" someone. It is, in fact, prideful, arrogant and self-serving.

- Stage 2 is when the relationship moves to admiration. You develop a genuine interest in who they are. You want to know them better. Perhaps you want to become more like them. You feel special when you are in their presence.

- The next stage is when spending time with that person becomes a priority in your life; you can open your heart and share everything. You take great delight in knowing them, loving them, caring for them and serving them. It is also important to demonstrate your love toward them.

- This ultimate friendship is laying your life down for another. Jesus gave us the perfect example; His greatest act of serving was to lay His life down when He died on the cross. We know what real love is because Jesus gave up his life for us. So we also ought to give up our lives for our brothers and sisters. —I John 3:16.[5]

I thank God for His abundance of patience with me through my stubbornness. Even as an adult I remained a spoiled brat until He, in His great love, began to discipline me. Our relationship continues to grow and deepen as long as I apply those consistent daily practices—reading the Word and cultivating our friendship. I have a greater awareness of Him being with me wherever I go and in whatever I am doing. God doesn't love me less when I let those practices slip, but I cease to grow when they do. I always want to go deeper into the things of the Spirit. I want to know Him better every day. I heard a speaker once say, "If you are not paddling upstream, you are floating backward."

Sometimes, one must aggressively pursue the Lord with strength and fortitude: you study Him like you would learn a subject in school. Read His Word or study material that enlarges your understanding of Him. Seek out those who understand His ways and sit under their teaching.

Seek out people or gatherings where God is free to move in the full measure of His Spirit. Learn the ways of the Spirit from being around those who are pursuing and functioning in them.

Giving your heart to the Lord Jesus doesn't mean that you are exempt from pain and struggles. In fact, the Word clearly says that we will have them. *Consider it pure joy, my brothers, whenever you face trials of many kinds.* —JAMES 1:2. In His great love, the Lord allows us to face difficulties. However, when Jesus is Lord of our life, we have a constant companion beside us, guiding and strengthening us through it.

JOHN 16:33—*I have told you these things, so that in me you may have peace. In this world you will have trouble. But take heart! I have overcome the world.*

ROMANS 8:28—*And we know that all things work together for the good to them that love God and are called according to His purpose.*

Nuggets of Truth:

I had no idea Jesus desired to have friendship with me.

Greater love has no one than this; that he lay down his life for his friends. You are my friends if you do what I command, I no longer call you servants, because a servant does not know his master's business. Instead, I have called you friends, for everything that I learned from my Father I have made known to you. —John 15: 13-15

That revelation changed everything for me. Before long I became comfortable with Him, and began having intimate conversations with Him day and night. The more our relationship grew, the more I fell in love with Him. My heart awakened to His kindness. Time and time again He showed me His unconditional acceptance and how He didn't measure me according to my past but according to who I am in Him.

After I learned that, I would spend hours just enjoying His presence. Even though I couldn't see Him, I felt Him next to me. It was like I was soaking in the rays of sun on a warm afternoon. Before that time, I had no idea I was so loved. His love radically changed me. As I surrendered myself and opened my heart to Him, He filled me with His Spirit. Then He began to teach me His ways and reveal His thoughts to me.

He who forms the mountains, creates the wind, and reveals his thoughts to man, he who turns dawn to darkness, and treads the high places of the earth— the LORD God Almighty is his name. —Amos 4:13

I began to realize since the Lord was speaking to me, He also speaks to every one else who listens to Him. Every Christian can hear the voice of the Lord. *The LORD confides in those who fear him; he makes his covenant known to them.* —Psalm 25:14

My sheep hear My voice, and I know them, and they follow Me. —John 10:27

Listening to the Lord requires exercising your "spiritual ears." Linger in quietness to hear Him speak. Listen with your Spirit, not with your mind. At some point, stop your flow of words and listen. Let Him speak with words of love and encouragement, wisdom and knowledge, instruction and direction. We will never hear Him if our mouth is constantly moving. It's like any other conversation. In order to listen, it is necessary to stop talking.

In times of waiting on Him, I don't pray, sing or study. I simply wait in silence. If you don't hear anything the first time, try again and again. Don't give up. Your spiritual ears have to be trained to hear. God speaks Spirit to spirit. He also speaks through His Word or through other people. But I believe He always speaks directly to those who have been trained to listen to His voice.

He is waiting to commune with us. Here I am! I stand at the door and knock. If anyone hears my voice and opens the door, I will come in and eat with him, and he with me. —Revelation 3:20

The more we wait on Him, the better we know Him and the more finely tuned we become to His voice. Give God space in your life and He *will* come and respond to you. Deuteronomy 4:29— *But if from there you seek the LORD your God, you will find him if you look for him with all your heart and with all your soul.*

As you learn to discern His voice, remember that the Lord will never say anything that contradicts His Word. If you're not sure that you heard Him correctly, ask Him for confirmation of what He said. Or, ask mature and trusted Christian leaders to help you discern His voice. If it was His voice speaking to you, He will confirm it.

*Later, the Lord sent this message to King Ahaz: "Ask the Lord your God for a sign of confirmation, Ahaz. Make it as difficult as you want—as high as heaven or as deep as the place of the dead." —*Isaiah 7:10-12.[6]

He understands the process of learning and will help you.

*But the Counselor, the Holy Spirit, whom the Father will send in my name, will teach you all things and will remind you of everything I have said to you. —*John 14:26

Meditation Questions

Take time to examine your heart and answer the following questions.

1. What does having a close friend mean to you? And in what stage of friendship is that relationship to you? (Refer to Content Point for friendship stages on page 9.)

_____

_____

_____

_____

2. Is God a friend to you? What kind of friend? Is your relationship growing deeper with Him?

_____

_____

_____

_____

3. Do you hear an "inner" voice and do you know it is the voice of the Lord speaking to you? For example, when you are making a decision about what to do or say, is the voice faithful to, and consistent with, the scriptures? What are some things that He has said to you?

_____

_____

_____

_____

4. Do you want to cultivate a better friendship with
   God? If so, what are you going to do to pursue that
   friendship?

_____

_____

_____

_____

Prayer

As you read this prayer, make it your own.

Dear Lord,

You have been a part of my life but not as much as You could be or as much as I want You to be. You are so much more than a friend...You have supreme authority and are also Lord of the universe. Now that I understand You long for a deeper relationship with me, I come in agreement with Your desire. I want to get to know You and for You to become real to me on a daily basis.

Please fill me with Your Spirit. Teach me Your ways and lead me in the paths of understanding. Deepen my passion for You so I can mature in wisdom.

Give me grace and strength to pursue You. Draw me close to your side for I desire to walk and talk with You throughout the day and be called Your friend. Help me be a good friend to You.

Thank you for making our relationship possible through Your Son. In Jesus' Name, Amen.

Additional Scripture References

I believe these scriptures will help you build a deeper friendship with the Lord:

Romans 5:18—*Yes, Adam's one sin brings condemnation for everyone, but Christ's one act of righteousness brings a right relationship with God and new life for everyone.* [7]

Luke 5:20—*When Jesus saw their faith, he said, "Friend, your sins are forgiven."*

James 2:23—*And so it happened just as the Scriptures say: "Abraham believed God, and God counted him as righteous because of his faith." He was even called the friend of God.*[8]

1 John 4:7—*Let us love one another, for love comes from God. Everyone who loves has been born of God and knows God.*

James 4:4— *Don't you know that if you love the world, you are God's enemies? And if you decide to be a friend of the world, you make yourself an enemy of God.*[9]

Exodus 34:14—*You must worship no other gods, for the Lord, whose very name is Jealous, is a God who is jealous about his relationship with you.*[10]

Luke 12:21— *"Yes, a person is a fool to store up earthly wealth but not have a rich relationship with God."* [11]

Romans 4:13—*Clearly, God's promise to give the whole earth to Abraham and his descendants was based not on his obedience to God's law, but on a right relationship with God that comes by faith.*[12]

2 John 1:9—*Anyone who wanders away from this teaching has no relationship with God. But anyone who remains in the teaching of Christ has a relationship with both the Father and the Son.*[13]

REVELATION 21:3— *And I heard a loud voice from the throne saying, "Now the dwelling of God is with men, and he will live with them. They will be his people, and God himself will be with them and be their God.*

Scripture to Memorize

ROMANS 5:11—*So now we can rejoice in our wonderful new relationship with God because our Lord Jesus Christ has made us friends of God.*

Endnotes

[2]Virgil P. Brock and Blanche Kerr Brock, Beyond the Sunset (Public domain).

[3]Scripture quotation taken from the Holy Bible, New Living Translation, copyright 1996, 2004. Used by permission of Tyndale House Publishers, Inc., Wheaton, Illinois 60189. All rights reserved.

[4]Scripture quotation taken from the Holy Bible, New Living Translation, copyright 1996, 2004. Used by permission of Tyndale House Publishers, Inc., Wheaton, Illinois 60189. All rights reserved.

[5]Scripture quotation taken from the Holy Bible, New Living Translation, copyright 1996, 2004. Used by permission of Tyndale House Publishers, Inc., Wheaton, Illinois 60189. All rights reserved.

[6]Scripture quotation taken from the Holy Bible, New Living Translation, copyright 1996, 2004. Used by permission of Tyndale House Publishers, Inc., Wheaton, Illinois 60189. All rights reserved.

[7]Scripture quotation taken from the Holy Bible, New Living Translation, copyright 1996, 2004. Used by permission of Tyndale House Publishers, Inc., Wheaton, Illinois 60189. All rights reserved.

[8]Ibid.

[9]Scripture taken from the Amplified Bible, Copyright © 1954, 1958, 1962, 1964, 1965, 1987 by The Lockman Foundation. Used by permission

[10]Scripture quotation taken from the Holy Bible, New Living Translation, copyright 1996, 2004. Used by permission of Tyndale House Publishers, Inc., Wheaton, Illinois 60189. All rights reserved.

[11]Ibid.

[12]Ibid.

[13]Ibid.

[14]Ibid.

Chapter 2

UNLIKELY PREDATORS

THE FIRST WEEK OF SUMMER WAS ALWAYS MY PEAK OF HAPPINESS. Each morning as the sun kissed the eastern horizon, I jumped out of bed to embrace another day of adventure with my brother Mark. We would ride our bicycles until hunger drove us back home for a meal. We zipped through narrow paths in the woods, over tree stumps and around rock ledges. Even getting slapped in the face by overgrown branches didn't slow us down in our race to the creek. If the water wasn't too deep, we continued peddling through it, trying to get to the other side without falling in. The creeks, and forest along the banks of the Mississippi made a wonderful land of adventure.

Although my brother had purchased a Honda 100 motorbike a year earlier, he still occasionally rode his bicycle with me. However, he often let me know he was doing me a huge favor because he much preferred his motorbike.

Before long he wanted a bigger bike. So that spring he bought a new Honda 350. From time to time, he let me take his little Honda 100 for a spin. I felt like such a grown up as I straddled the black leather seat and stomped on the kick-start. Instantly the motor rumbled and I was flying down the road. On rare occasion, Mark let me switch with him so I could see how cool his new motorcycle was. He always prefaced the privilege with a stern warning, "Be careful now. It has a lot more power than my other bike, so don't wreck it." And boy, was he right! As I gave it the gas, I was instantly addicted to the extra horsepower.

Early one July morning in 1972, my parents left town for a meeting in Kansas City. Since they would only be gone for a couple of days, and we had many friends and family nearby, they decided to let us stay home alone. Mark was seventeen and I was fifteen.

That same day, my boyfriend Bill and his buddy roared into town on two brand-new motorcycles they had just driven off the showroom floor. When he pulled up next to me, the machine shook the ground. The vibration of Bill's new Kawasaki 750 pulsed through my body. I loved it.   Even though we weren't *officially* dating, Bill and I were infatuated with each other. Stolen kisses in the parking lot after church made it feel official. His dad pastored a church across the Mississippi River from Pontoosuc, in nearby Ft. Madison, Iowa. He occasionally dropped by to see me after his church dismissed on Sunday night. Since he was five years older than me and appeared responsible, dad usually let him escort me to special church events.

I'm not sure what charmed me more, seeing my boyfriend or his new bike. The spotless shimmer of gold and blue enamel caught my eye like a fishing lure attracting a trout. I was fascinated with the huge metal machine! I wanted to ride it. I could almost feel how, at the snap of my wrist, it would cut through the wind in a split second.

As Bill explained all the fancy levers and described its incredibly smooth ride, my excitement rose. I fearlessly begged to take it for a spin. After much persistent cuteness, he gave in to my pleading. Throwing my leg over the bike, I raced the purring engine. I could tell it was much heavier than any bike I had ridden before. He carefully showed me where the brakes and gearshift were, and warned me to take it easy until I had the feel of it. I slowly let out the clutch and raced away!

As soon as I turned the corner and was out of his sight, I opened it full throttle and hit 60 miles per hour. What a rush! It was going to be a short joy ride though. I had six blocks before I had to make the sharp curve at the end of the street. A boat ramp into the river was waiting for me if I didn't.

Hair whipping in the wind and grinning from ear to ear, I felt invincible. Actually, I might have been invincible if a black streak had not come lunging at the bike from a nearby yard. All of a sudden I felt a jolt and heard a yelp as my front tire hit a snarling dog. Since I hadn't seen it coming, I didn't slow down or brace my arms for the impact. The collision immediately flipped the bike on its side. Still clinging to the handlebars, I was trapped under the bike as gravel and dust pounded my face and body. Half a block later, I slid to a stop. The dog was dead and I wasn't sure that I was not far behind him.

Bill and his friend heard the crash blocks away and came running. Neighbors came out from their houses and couldn't believe what they saw. There, in a cloud of dust and metal, a body moved. I was still alive!

Rushing to my rescue, they lifted the mangled bike. The weight of that once-beautiful machine had crushed my left side. Blood and tears were running down my face. I didn't know if I was crying because of my injuries or that I had crashed Bill's brand new bike. I kept repeating, "I am so sorry…oh my gosh, I am so sorry." Bill tried to comfort me, "Don't worry about it. It can be fixed. Let's just get you to the hospital right now." That's all I remember until I woke up in the Emergency Room.

I was still disoriented when the ER doctor appeared with my chart. When he closed the curtain behind him, I immediately felt uneasy. Even though I had never been in a hospital before, somehow I knew physician etiquette required a nurse to be present before an exam. But we were alone and he was not waiting for anyone before proceeding.

As he lifted my gown, he tried to calm me by saying, "I am simply going to examine your cuts and bruises to evaluate your condition." At first, his purpose seemed legitimate. But as he continued, I knew he was no longer inspecting my wounds. I was quite sure I was not injured in the area he was examining or the way he was touching me.

I couldn't believe what was happening. He was molesting me. The audacity; he was supposed to be a professional helping me, not taking advantage of me! As the realization sank in, I got mad. With my uninjured right hand I grabbed his arm and said, "Stop it!" He calmly said, "It's OK; this will make you feel better." But that just made me angrier. Suddenly, I could no longer feel the pain. With all the strength I could muster, I rose up on the gurney and yelled, "If you don't stop it, I'm going to scream. Now get out of here!" Startled by my assertiveness, he stopped and immediately left the room. Soon, a female nurse came in to dress the wounds where the skin on the left side of my face and body was torn away. I was so shaken by what had just happened, I laid there in complete silence.

The hospital was in Fort Madison, Iowa, about ten miles from Pontoosuc. But, still, several hours later, no one was with me in the Emergency Room. I couldn't figure out where everyone was. I felt so alone. Trying to be strong, I fought back the tears. Finally, I asked the nurse to dial Bill's number for me. When he answered, I started to cry. Stuttering through the tears, I whispered, "The doctor has molested me!" I pleaded, "Would you please come and sit with me at the hospital? I don't want him to come back."

I was shocked when he replied, "No, I can't come tonight. You'll be fine." Then he added, "A doctor would never do a thing like that. It must have been your imagination." I felt suffocated, like a pillow had been placed over my face. How could he ignore my cry for help? I was stunned at his lack of compassion. His response crossed over the line of human decency. He was a fool not to come to me in my desperate time of need!

My heart went cold as I hung up the phone. It was clear he wasn't man enough to help me in my greatest time of trouble. That was it! The romance was over.

My parents arrived from Kansas City the next day. I was so happy and relieved to be embraced by someone who cared! I cried and cried as they held me. Of course, they had no idea that most of my tears were because of what the doctor did to me. I could never bring myself to tell them everything.

Mom never understood why I was so stressed every time we went to see that doctor for follow up visits. I made her promise never to leave the room while he changed my dressings. They often wondered why his office never charged for the hospitalization or the months of follow up appointments with him. I understood! He was guilty and he knew it. If I breathed a word of what had happened in the hospital room, he could be prosecuted.

The doctor said I would always have scars on the left side of my face, hands and body where the gravel road had torn away the flesh. In fact, he was not able to remove all the gravel. My parents weren't willing to accept his report and began to pray. Within one year there was no sign I had ever had an accident! My skin healed beautifully and was completely normal.

God healed the bruises and scars on my body, but I also had scars on my heart. The pain of sexual violation by a trusted authority and the pain of abandonment soon began to fade. At least, I thought it did. I tried to bury the trauma by plunging all my attention and energy back into school, family, and church life…and it seemed to work most of the time.

A year later, on a warm summer night, I agreed to meet up with some of my cousins and their friends at the river front park. I never knew what would happen when we got together; we were fairly rowdy. All of us had grown up in Christian homes but we didn't always act like it. Many times we were as buck wild as all the other kids in town.

One of my cousins, Jason, had just bought a brand new red Corvette and he was showing it off by racing the engine to impress everyone. We gathered around, smelling the leather seats, and caressing its beauty. Jason was a handsome guy and he knew it. Heads always turned when he walked by. He impressed the girls. After a while, he came over to me and said, "Hey, Leann, do you want to take a ride in my new car?"

"Sure," I said, thrilled that he asked me to go for a ride. Feeling cocky, I stepped in to the car. I was going to "drag the strip" with the "hottest" guy and car in town. Even though he *was* my cousin, I idolized his suave debonair. "Come on, let's go," I said. Pulling away from the crowd I felt elated that I had been the one he chose to parade around in his new wheels. As we cruised the streets of the small town, we waved and honked at his school buddies loitering on the sidewalks. I felt like I had just crossed over into a new league of "cool" just by sitting next to him.

Everything was perfect as the radio blasted, vibrating the door panels. The "new car" aroma brought an endorphin rush. With every breath, I floated deeper into a fantasy world and thought, "This is what it must feel like to be a wealthy society chick hanging out with handsome important people." Driving under the streetlights, I felt like I was on a movie set. As I wiggled back into the leather seats, I congratulated myself thinking, "If my friends could see me now, I would be catapulted to a whole new elite status!" What a moment!

As we drew near the edge of town Jason said, "Would you like to see what this big engine can do on the open road?"

"Sure, let me see what it's got." As he accelerated, the G-force pressed me further back into the seat and the wind whipped through my hair. Within seconds, we were flying down the road, way over the speed limit. Just about the time I was getting nervous, he took his foot off the gas.

At first, I thought he was slowing down to make a U-turn to head back into town. Instead, he turned onto a gravel road and continued driving. When I asked where we were going, he said, "Oh, I just want to show you something down here." I wasn't worried or afraid because I was always up for an adventure. However, I couldn't imagine what he was going to show me in the dark. He wouldn't tell me what it was but kept assuring me it was really going to be worth the surprise.

We rounded a bend in the road and turned onto a grassy area

and stopped. He turned off the lights. I asked, "What are we doing here?" Still waiting for the surprise, I sat there looking around. He seemed a little nervous, then suddenly leaned over the console, grabbed me and pulled me closer. "Come here," he demanded and started kissing me. I tried to push him away.

Even though he had been drinking, I wasn't afraid of him. I thought for sure I could talk him out of his sexual encroachment, but I quickly found out no amount of talking was going to stop him. He was ruthlessly determined to have his way. Since he outweighed me by about a hundred pounds and was very muscular, I wasn't able to fight him off and there was no need to scream for help. We were in the middle of nowhere. As soon as he finished with me, he let me go. I opened the door and rolled out on the cool grass. Screaming through my tears, I yelled,

"I can't believe you just did that! You jerk! Are you crazy? What is wrong with you? You #X!#@)*&! God, what if I get pregnant? What are you going to do if that happens, huh? How's that going to look to our family?" He was silent.

Mad as a hornet, I got up and pulled my clothes back together. Finally, I got back into the car and shouted, "Take me back to town!"

As we drove back to town, my mind raged, "How could I have been so stupid to trust him?" What started out to be a perfectly innocent joy ride ended in disgusting defilement. I was furious with him but also mad at myself. I felt like such an idiot! In those few entangled moments, my fantasy "elite status" was reduced to a dirty dark secret.

I was so relieved to see the town lights emerging in the distance. I couldn't wait to get away from Jason and out of his hellhole on wheels. All I wanted was to get home. It was late when I walked through the door. Shaking from head to toe, I was glad everyone had gone to bed. I could not have possibly explained being so disheveled and raw with emotion. Desperately wanting to wash away the disgusting memory, I ran to the bathroom and shut the door. I felt so terribly alone. No one knew about the nasty secret except God. He was the only one I could turn to. Tormented, I suffered through the night. Soaking my pillow, I cried, "I am so sorry, God. Please forgive me…I don't want to get pregnant, Please God! Help me!"

For days, I was quiet and withdrawn. My inner struggle consumed every thought. I couldn't imagine ever facing Jason again. I decided if I didn't get pregnant, no one would ever have to know. The last thing I wanted was a vicious feud to tear our families apart.

I was so relieved when my monthly cycle came a few weeks later! Somehow the darkness of being raped grew lighter just knowing there wasn't going to be a baby to further complicate the situation. Now it was just between the Lord and me. I knew He was the only one who could take away the shame.

Over the next two years, I tried to avoid family gatherings. When I couldn't, I left the room if Jason appeared. Then one day, I had a revelation. The only one suffering from this awful pain was *me*. My rapist seemed to be living a very happy and carefree life. He didn't appear to have any remorse or even memory of that dreadful night.

Finally, I said to myself, "I have to get over the bitterness of being raped by my cousin and molested by a doctor!" What would stop my seething anger at them? I desperately needed to be free of the resentment because it was eating me alive. I literally hated them for what they had done to me but felt powerless to do anything about it. I wanted revenge, but I knew that the scriptures say, "Vengeance is mine, saith the Lord." I thought, *if I let God take care of it maybe He will kill them for me.* In my vindictive state of mind, there could be nothing better than to rid the earth of two more perverts.

One day, I got sick and tired of wallowing in self-pity, so I sat down and had a long serious talk with myself. "OK, Leann, you need to get a grip here. What was done to you didn't kill you and you didn't get pregnant. Thank God for that! Now, you have to let go of your hatred and let God take away your pain so you can move on. Permitting those horrible events to steal every quiet moment, and living under a cloud of depression is not adding one thing to your life. You are nothing but a miserable and unhappy eighteen-year-old. You have allowed the demons of torment to completely rule you."

I had a choice to make. I could hang on to the pain as a trophy of self-pity or let go of it. I knew I wasn't capable of changing anyone else, so I was the one who would have to change. I needed rescuing from my invisible lonely prison. I knew I had to grow up and face what must be done.

As I waited for the Lord to help me, He revealed something very important. I had asked Him to forgive *me* but I had never asked Him to forgive them or help me to forgive *them*. I then asked the Lord to forgive them and to give me the grace to forgive them as well.

I didn't want any residue of resentment left in my mind or my heart, so I asked Him to *renew* my thoughts toward those men. I asked Him to forgive me for hating them and fill me with His love. I desperately wanted the scripture, *Love covers all wrongs* (PROVERBS 10:12) to become the reality I had not yet experienced.

As I prayed, God met me. It was amazing; as soon as I took the offenses down from the pedestal of importance and put God back into that place, the pain left. Finally, I was set free from the pain of my past. With His help, I let it go. The depression left, the voices of torment stopped and I felt alive once again!

APPLICATION STUDY GUIDE

Week Two [Date: _____]

Pick one day out of your week when you can take time to sit and reflect on the following thoughts and respond to the meditation questions below.

Second Key To Becoming Free: *Forgive yourself and others.*

Sometimes terrible things happen to us, or those we love, that are simply beyond our control. Many times we didn't even see them coming. But, even if we could have, *or did*, we cannot change it after the fact. It happened. That's why it's imperative to understand and live under God's grace and forgiveness. Not only for others but for ourselves.

Always keep in mind that we have an enemy, Satan, who is always hard at work to destroy us.

A thief comes to steal and kill and destroy, but I came to give life—life in all its fullness. —John 10:10

In one way or another, the enemy's goal is to violate us physically, emotionally or spiritually in an attempt to disfigure our emotions so that we are crippled for the rest of our life. Typically, he begins his attempts to devastate us when we are tender and innocent children. He wants to get us messed up and handicapped when we're young, helpless, afraid, or unable to distinguish right from wrong.

Those are Satan's plans, not God's. The second part of John 10:10—"I have come to give you life, life to it's fullest"—is what God plans to do. Even when the enemy breaches the boundary of protection, the situation does not become hopeless. God will rescue and redeem us.

He never promised we would go through life without difficulties, but He did promise this: "When you go through deep waters, I will be with you. When you go through rivers of dif-

ficulty, you will not drown. When you walk through the fire of oppression, you will not be burned up; the flames will not consume you."—ISAIAH 43:2[15]

I wish I could understand why God allows certain things to happen to people. It doesn't seem fair to my human mind. In my situation, I couldn't understand what I did to deserve such a crime. It took a long time to realize I just happened to be at the wrong place at the wrong time. Wounded people wound other people and I was just another victim. In fact, we live in a fallen world where bad things happen.

But the good news is, even when evil touches our lives, we don't have to give up. We can pick up, start over and move on. God will turn it around for our good and make it work beautifully as a part of His great plan. Even when we get wounded, He is always there, reaching out to heal us with His love and comfort.

The Lord not only allowed me to go through those traumatic events, but let me stay in my misery until I was ready to let go of it. Only then did He come to my rescue. As soon as I allowed Him to touch my needs, the Great Physician healed my heart.

Nuggets of Truth

No matter what we have experienced, no matter who was at fault, and no matter how dirty, ugly or shameful it was—God still loves us. Nothing will ever change that fact. His love for us is complete, guaranteed, and without limitations. Nothing can separate us from His love. Nothing.

For I am convinced that neither death nor life, neither angels nor demons, neither the present nor the future, nor any powers, neither height nor depth, nor anything else in all creation, will be able to separate us from the love of God that is in Christ Jesus our Lord. —ROMANS 8:38-39

The Lord will let us simmer in the tormented emotions of our experience until we are ready to deal with it and let it go. The longer an issue is not dealt with, the harder it is to get rid of it. The roots of bitterness grow deeper, and are often forgotten, until we remember the person or event that hurt us. Then suddenly, as the pain comes flooding back into our consciousness, we realize there are unresolved issues.

Unfortunately, because some people find comfort in the familiar pain of an offense, they prefer to hang on to their wounded state. Each time they relive it, they allow themselves to indulge in self-pity and the sympathy it brings from others. In doing so, they forfeit their healing because it satisfies a need for attention.

It is critical to our spiritual health and vitality to let go of the wounds from the past. If we do not, the past will shape our future through distorted memories and expectations; it will shape our perspective of who we are and Who God is. Without change, our viewpoint remains warped and twisted. We must embrace the lessons to be learned and let go of the trauma. If we do not allow the blood of Jesus and His forgiveness to cover our past, Satan will continue to have access into our lives.

Always remember that the Lord is not hard on us. Not ever. At times we are, but He never is. Just as a parent loves his or her child far more than the child could possibly love himself, Jesus loves us far more than we love ourselves.

I will never forget those events, but there is no longer pain attached to their memory. A blanket of love fell over them when I forgave. As unbelievable as it may sound, I feel compassion, not hate, toward those who violated me. Because I'm not looking through my pain anymore, I see those men through different eyes…God's eyes. He loves them greatly.

NOTE: One out of every three women in the US is a victim of a sex crime at some point in their life. If you are a victim, don't deal with it alone. First, report the incident to authorities like I wish I had done. At the time, I didn't have the courage to do that. Thank God, today's judicial system is equipped and committed to protect victims and stop predators from repeat crimes. Take advantage of their help. Also tell someone you trust—preferably a licensed professional—and allow him or her to help you get through the emotional and physical trauma of your situation.

Meditation Questions

Take time to examine your heart and fill in the answers.

- Have you ever been assaulted physically, mentally or sexually? By one or more people? Describe the situation(s). Name the violator(s). Are you still living with the pain or natural consequences from the violations?

_____

_____

_____

_____

- How has it affected your life?

_____

_____

_____

_____

- Are you ready to be free from the torment of it? Even though it may seem impossible to you, it is certainly not impossible for God.

_____

_____

_____

_____

Prayer

As you read this prayer, make it your own. If there is more than one name on your list, pray through the prayer with one name at a time.

Dear Lord Jesus, You see the path I have walked and You see the pain I bear. I know it is not Your will that I carry the wounds and unfair treatment of (name the trauma)_____ from my past. So I humble myself to say, I am ready to give the pain of (name of the trauma)_____ to You and let it go. I don't want to keep those memories in my personal "prison of unforgiveness" anymore. I want to be free of the pain.

Lord, I ask that You forgive (name of the offender) _____ who wronged me. Also, give me the grace to forgive them for I know it is Your will that I be free of any resentment or grievance against another person. Even though Satan tried to entangle me with bitterness and anger, I choose to let go of it and I choose to trust you to come to my defense. Where I have been wronged, please make it right. As I let go of the offense, I am releasing You to deal with (name of the offender)_____.

(Declare this next statement out loud)
"I forgive you, (name of the offender) _____, in Jesus' Name."
And Lord, have mercy on (name of the offender) _____, as You have had on me.

Lord, I also ask that You allow me to see through Your eyes and give me Your heart towards (name of the offender) _____. I need Your grace to complete this process of healing. From now on, I want to be able to respond to them as You would. I need Your strength to stand as one who does not pronounce judgment on others but one who extends grace, kindness and love. Use me as a catalyst of peace in this relationship.

Lord, You have already forgiven me and paid the price for my sin and pain on the cross. You hold nothing against me, so today I forgive myself as well. I am no longer going to be angry and disappointed with myself. I am letting it all go right now. Your Word says You have removed my transgressions from me as far as the east is from the west and You remember them no more. I declare who You say I am....I am Your child and I am the righteousness of God in Christ. Thank you, Lord, for coming to my rescue and healing my heart to make me whole again. In Jesus' Name, Amen.

Additional Scripture References

Please take time to read these scriptures. They confirm that the Lord loves you and wants you to walk in peace and freedom through forgiveness. Just as He forgave us, we must forgive others.

LEVITICUS 19:18— *Do not seek revenge or bear a grudge against one of your people, but love your neighbor as yourself. I am the LORD.*

ROMANS 12:19— *Do not take revenge, my friends, but leave room for God's wrath, for it is written: "It is mine to avenge; I will repay," says the Lord.*

PSALM 32:1— *Blessed is he whose transgressions are forgiven, whose sins are covered.*

PSALM 103:2-5— *Praise the LORD, O my soul, and forget not all his benefits, who forgives all your sins and heals all your diseases, who redeems your life from the pit and crowns you with love and compassion, who satisfies your desires with good things so that your youth is renewed like the eagle's.*

MATTHEW 6:12— *And forgive us our sins, as we have forgiven those who sin against us.*[16]

HEBREWS 8:12— *For I will forgive their wickedness and will remember their sins no more.*

Numbers 14:18— *The LORD is slow to anger, abounding in love and forgiving sin and rebellion.*

Psalm 31:7— *I will be glad and rejoice in your love, for you saw my affliction and knew the anguish of my soul.*

Psalm 44:26— *Rise up and help us; redeem us because of your unfailing love.*

Psalm 103:12— *He has taken our sins away from us as far as the east is from west.*[17]

Matthew 26:28— *This is my blood of the covenant, which is poured out for many for the forgiveness of sins.*

Additional Reference Books on Forgiveness

The Healing Presence: Curing the Soul Through Union with Christ by Leanne Payne (Baker Books, 1995)

The Broken Image: Restoring Personal Wholeness Through Healing Prayer by Leanne Payne (Baker Books, 1995)

Forgiveness by John Arnott (Chosen Books, 2003)

Scripture to Memorize

Colossians 3:13 (NIV)—*Bear with each other and forgive whatever grievances you may have against one another. Forgive as the Lord forgave you.*

Endnotes

[15]Scripture quotation taken from the Holy Bible, New Living Translation, copyright 1996, 2004. Used by permission of Tyndale House Publishers, Inc., Wheaton, Illinois 60189. All rights reserved.

[16]Scripture quotation taken from the Holy Bible, New Living Translation, copyright 1996, 2004. Used by permission of Tyndale House Publishers, Inc., Wheaton, Illinois 60189. All rights reserved.

[17]Scriptures quoted from The Holy Bible, New Century Version, copyright © 1987, 1988, 1991 by Word Publishing, Nashville, Tennessee. Used by permission

Chapter 3
RESISTING THE AGE OF IMAGE

AT EIGHT YEARS OLD, I RIPPED OPEN THE CHRISTMAS PAPER and gasped with delight at the green-hinged case. My anticipation jumped when I saw the words "Miss Suzette" and four beautiful Barbie dolls painted on the lid. Scanning their flawless features, I noticed each painted doll was so voluptuous. Their curvaceous figures were enhanced with stunning designer wear. Their exquisite slender legs stood in dainty high heels and their faces were framed with long flowing locks of hair that seemed delicately tousled by the wind.

I could hardly believe my eyes! Was I awake this Christmas morning or was I dreaming? If I was awake, could I trust what was painted on the outside of the case? Sometimes we got Christmas presents wrapped in old boxes so we never knew what was really on the inside until we opened them. I was almost afraid to unlatch it. I didn't want to be disappointed and find something other than a Barbie doll.

Unable to stand the suspense any longer, I lifted the latch and the case flew open like a Jack-in-the-Box. The plastic smell of a freshly manufactured dolly filled the air. I wasn't dreaming. As I pushed aside the mountain of designer wear, there she was. I let out a shriek.

I had never seen anything so beautiful in my whole life! Stacked on either side the window box in which she stood, drawers opened up into a dressing room. Every outfit hung on color-coordinated hangers. She even came with her own stand so I could display her beauty on my dresser when we finished playing.

Until that Christmas, I had only played with my friends' Barbie dolls. I always hated to leave them behind when I went home.

Now—the doll I held in my hands would make that sadness go away forever. I blurted out, "This is the best Christmas ever! I finally have my very own Barbie doll! She's mine... all mine. Thank you, Grandma!" With twinkling eyes, she smiled back and said, "You're welcome, honey."

Miss Suzette was a brunette, just like me; but she was very grown up. Since my grandmother was gifted at sewing and knitting, she made Miss Suzette an entire wardrobe of exquisite clothes for her boudoir, complete with matching hats and shoes. She had plenty of outfits for every season of the year!

As a child, playing with dolls was my favorite pastime. Getting a dolly for Christmas was a rare event and I treasured each one of them. In addition to my new Barbie, I had a green stuffed floppy-eared dog that I slept with. I also had a life-sized baby doll and a hard plastic troll with wiry blonde hair. The troll was perfect for the times I didn't feel very girlish. He and I went to war with my brother's toys. Occasionally, he got catapulted across the bed, hitting the floor with every hair still in place.

I so enjoyed Miss Suzette's company. We lived in an imaginary world together, lost in conversation about shopping, going to church, or some romantic encounter with her invisible suitors. She was a high fashion chick with a very demanding social calendar. Because she was so particular about her appearance, Miss Suzette insisted on being glamorously presentable at all times. Even when she went to the grocery store, she was impeccable with matching accessories and high heels. She was simply beautiful.

I loved to change her clothes for each of her high society appearances. I couldn't help but notice her curvy molded figure. I always thought: *Someday, I want to be as perfect as she is. When I walk through a doorway, I want my beauty to turn heads and command attention like she does.* From those early impressions, an image of perfection became etched indelibly in my mind.

As a teenager, I noticed fashion magazines and billboards portraying the female body as an object of worship. Even then, the culture presented sexy bodies selling everything from toothpaste to sports cars. Those models reminded me of Miss Suzette.

As I started Dallas City High School in Illinois, my desire to be model-beautiful became an obsession. I didn't want to be ignored like unattractive girls. In fact, many times it was hard to concentrate on my studies because I was trying to get the attention of the boys.

To me, beauty assured that one would be desired and loved. Any high school "trophy beauty" had great worth; all the kids in school talked about them. The guys were willing to make every sacrifice to win her affection. In high school, it seemed the ultimate reward for a boy was to walk through the school hallways with her—his prized possession—dangling from his arm.

When I graduated from High School, my beloved grandmother passed away and we moved to St. Louis. I missed her terribly. She left a big hole in my life because I took refuge in her genuine love. She also left a small inheritance that my parents shared with Mark and me. As they gave me a handful of brand new bills, they said, "First of all, don't forget to tithe a tenth of it to the Lord, and secondly, take your time and spend it wisely." Eight hundred dollars seemed like a million dollars to me. With that money I could finally put wings to my dream!

I decided to become a model. With grandma's money, and a little of my own, I signed up for Barbizon School of Modeling in St Louis. I knew the advantage of professional training in finishing school would put me one step closer to my dream: being a talking, living, and breathing "Miss Suzette."

I was in for a surprise the first week of school. I had no idea it took so much work to be beautiful! To me, "makeup" was powder on the nose to stop the shine on the way to church. "Skin care" was a soapy washcloth once a day. "Toner" was something we used in High School for film processing. I had never heard of body exfoliation. Everything was foreign to me. I couldn't understand why I had to first strip the skin of oil, and then apply moisturizer to replenish it. I had no idea there were so many steps to complete the facial cleansing process *before* make-up was ever applied.

The make-up artist introduced me to under eye concealer, no-crease eye shadow foundation, and powders that shade and others that highlight. I also learned about anti-feathering creams to keep lipstick framed. I had always applied everything with one powder puff, but at Barbizon, I quickly learned that every step of application had it's own brush, tailored with varied tips to complete the flawless "look."

When the instructor finished with me, I hardly recognized the person staring back at me from the mirror. The only other time I had seen anyone with that much make-up, was on a lady in a casket. My hair was coiffed and every pore was buffed for the "showing." I liked the change, but I didn't like all the fuss it took to get there. Good grief!

I learned how models on magazine covers appear absolutely perfect. It took hours of preparation and an entourage of artists to look that good! Soon, I started working on my own photo composites and found other tricks of the trade. The photographer took my pictures with lighted umbrellas and reflectors to create the softest complexion and skin tone. And if that didn't create a perfect image, a graphic artist erased blemishes, cellulite and trimmed off excess inches, simply with the sweep of a hand.

I also learned the correct ways to sit and stand; good posture was essential in the overall appearance. They also taught us how to glide on the runway and the angles of movement the photographers like best. At times, it was overwhelming. However, because I wanted to be a supermodel, I forged ahead.

At five-foot-nine, I was the right height to be a supermodel, but every week they reminded me I needed to loose more weight. I couldn't graduate until I lost a total of twenty-five pounds. I decided to get serious and do what I had to do to get it off. I was already working out every day but the pounds weren't coming off fast enough, so I decided to start cutting calories. A thousand calories a day seemed to work until I hit another plateau. With only three months left till graduation, I knew I had to get rid of those last stubborn pounds. Desperate, I started looking for other options. Even if it was drastic…you know, "Drastic results require drastic measures."

An acquaintance gave me some diet pills called "uppers." She said they would do the trick. I didn't want to take them because I had seen people strung out on drugs. For all I knew, their addiction could have started by innocently popping pills to shed a few pounds. But, one desperate day, I took a pill. It did exactly what she said it would do. I lost my appetite and I was revved to the max. I couldn't sleep for two whole days. After finally winding down, I realized messing with drugs and altering my body's chemistry was too risky.

I remembered a conversation from high school. Someone said, "I eat a meal, then throw it up. That way my body doesn't have to count the calories." It seemed like a repulsive and unnatural method of dieting, but I was desperate. The first time I tried it was totally disgusting! I stuck my finger down my throat and vomited every thing I had just eaten. The putrid smell and sight of regurgitated food floating in the toilet was nauseating. It was so repulsive that I could have hurled again had there been anything left to come up. Soon, I was able to mentally block the revulsion of it. Before long, I got hooked on the reward as the pounds began to melt away.

I had never heard the word "bulimia;" I just thought I was being clever. No drugs and my secret "diet" was easy to hide. Of course, at times I became desperately hungry. But, I really liked the new freedom of not counting calories. I could eat anything I wanted and kept loosing weight. I could binge on ice cream, cake, cookies and junk food and it didn't matter.

But as time went on, my mealtimes became increasingly emotional. I felt guilty with each bite of delicious food that mom had prepared. I began to hate myself for being so wasteful. Because I was loosing so much weight, people began to ask if I was sick. No one knew my dirty little secret and I intended to keep it that way! I knew I was declining but I was going to be skinny and no one was going to stop me! And besides, I only had two more weeks before graduation, and then I could stop my nasty routine.

One evening, after a wonderful meal with my family, something strange happened. Suddenly, what I had just eaten started coming up involuntarily! I jumped up, ran to the bathroom, shut the door, and hovered over the toilet. Now I was scared! This hideous habit was seeking to overpower me. Throwing up after every meal forced my body to change its natural digestive response. I had taught it to refuse food. Horrified, I realized that if I didn't stop purging, I might never again be able keep food down.

As I stood there terrified, a new strength rose up in me. Suddenly I became angry, not only with myself but also that Satan had fooled me into believing there would be no consequence for the abuse I was inflicting on my body. And I knew I was not alone in the bathroom. I could feel another force beside me; I felt like it was waiting to possess me and steal my right to feed my own body. I turned to the mirror, pointed my finger and declared to the unseen demonic presence, "You will never control me…no one and nothing will ever control me! Now leave in Jesus' name!" Then, that dark presence left the room.

When graduation day arrived, I had one last interview with my counselor at Barbizon. I walked into his office so proud of myself for achieving the goal of one hundred and twenty pounds. I thought I looked pretty hot; I was surely ready for the big time. As I told him the good news, he didn't even smile. He looked up and coldly said, "Come back when you get to one hundred and eighteen pounds and then I'll look at some agencies in New York for you." In disbelief I shrieked, "Two pounds!! You want me to loose two more pounds before you will try to get work for me?" Without explanation, he nodded and silently continued with the paperwork sitting in front of him.

As I turned around and walked out the door, the blood raced through my veins and anger flushed my face! I had tried so hard to be perfect and had done everything they told me to do. I had passed all the written exams, interviews, and runway tests. The school's contractual agreement was to get work for the graduates in New York or Los Angeles, and now a measly two pounds stood between the runway and me.

Graduation that night was not the celebration I thought it would be. As I received my diploma, I decided modeling was not for me. My body was simply not made to be pencil thin. I thought, "If that's what it takes to be a high fashion model, then someone else can have the job!" As much as I wanted it, the sacrifice was too great. I was no longer willing to obsess over every calorie to make modeling a career. Furthermore, "emaciated" was not a flattering look for me; I happened to like curves and flesh on my bones! Cooking, eating and exploring new flavors were great pleasures to me. There was more to life than a plate of raw broccoli and lemon water! I couldn't eat any less or work out any more! I was exhausted from the mental and physical pursuit of being skinny and oh, I was so very hungry!

Week Three   [Date: _____]

Pick one day out of your week when you can take time to sit and reflect on the following thoughts and respond to the meditation questions below.

Third Key To Becoming Free: *Allow God to Break the Power of Darkness Over Your Life.*

Looking back, I can clearly see that my desire to be a model was motivated by an unhealthy perception. I did not realize how much our culture shouts at us about outer beauty. Unless God builds character on the inside, we will be as artificial as a plastic Barbie doll.

In His great love for me, the Lord saved me from my shallow goals; He didn't allow all my wishes to come true because He knew they would destroy me.

At Barbizon, I saw the all-consuming obsession for physical beauty, the clawing for position at the top, and the lack of respect for others. Suddenly, the blinders fell off my eyes and my perspective changed. I saw that life is so much more than image or appearance.

Time has a way of sifting, rearranging, proving, and establishing what's important in life. I don't know what course my life would have taken had I become a supermodel. I'm just glad He revealed what was right for me and rescued me from deception.

If your chosen career and lifestyle do not permit you to be *you*, inquire deeply and earnestly about where that image of yourself came from! Who planted that in your mind? Trust me; you can be absolutely real with the Lord and He wants you to be *you*….. not someone else.

Nuggets of Truth

My husband teases me about how I've changed my opinion concerning styles. My new motto, "If you're ruled by fashion, you've got no guts." I simply mean, be yourself. Be objective about what looks good on your body type and wear it well...whether it's the hottest, latest, greatest style or not.

Our liberal society accentuates the "sensuous," which is a pre-occupation with bodily or sexual pleasures. It seeks to annihilate the "virtuous," which is moral excellence; right actions and thinking; goodness; strength. It's fine to allow current styles to influence what you wear. However, it saddens me to see people caught up in trends that desperately attract the wrong kind of attention. Our clothing choices should be modest, not implying or hinting at something rude or sexually improper. Simply put, "classy" always trumps "trashy." Incidentally, this applies to guys and girls alike.

We can't change the whole planet but we can change how our choices of fashion affect those around us. What we wear or don't wear speaks volumes about who we are. Good taste, class, elegance, grace, sophistication, and refinement in appearance not only gain respect, but should also mirror and compliment the beauty of our heart. Dressing properly reflects a godly confidence, dignity and security in who you are.

NOTE: Eating disorders and other addictions can be fatal if ignored. PLEASE seek professional counseling or someone who can stand with you in your decision to be free, support you in prayer and bring accountability.

Meditation Questions

Take time to examine your heart and fill in the answers. If the following questions do not pertain to you, put in the name of someone who struggles with addictions and pray for them.

- Have you ever been preoccupied with image? Do you obsess about physical appearance, money, or the kind of car your drive? Do you believe that fulfilling that image will bring you admiration, popularity, opportunities and ultimately, happiness? Give examples.

_____

_____

_____

_____

- Did this image pursuit lead to compromising or addictive behavior such as binging or starving, drinking, drugs, gambling or overworking, etc.? Explain what happened or is still happening.

_____

_____

_____

_____

- Does it still have control of your life? Can you see that outward appearances don't need to rule and preoccupy your life?

_____

_____

_____

_____

- Are you ready to break its power over you and let God take it away? When you are ready, pray the following prayer of deliverance.

_____

_____

_____

_____

_____

Prayer

As you read this prayer, make it your own.

Jesus, I want to live a life that honors You in every way. I realize I have been living in a state of existence that is far below Your best for me. I have allowed Satan to influence my choices and I have compromised my convictions.

I confess that I want to be set free from the power and control of this desire (name it) _____ over my life. Your Word says that if we resist Satan, in Jesus name, he must flee. So right now, Jesus, I ask that You deliver me from (name it) _____ that has kept me enslaved. Therefore, I speak with the authority You have given me in your wonderful name. Satan, GO, IN JESUS NAME! You have no right over my life. I am a child of God. Do not ever return again.

Lord, from now on, please help me to recognize when Satan tempts me; give me the strength and courage to resist him in Your name, Jesus. Your power is greater than any force that would seek to steal, kill and destroy my life. Now that Satan's power is broken, fill me with Your peace and healing. Lead me on a path of constructive behavior that will help me to grow into the person You designed me to be.

Finally, Lord, I ask that You would send guardian angels to keep watch over me and protect this new established place of victory. Thank You, Jesus for coming to my rescue and breaking the demonic strongholds over my life today. In Jesus' Name, Amen.

Additional Scripture References

Take time to read these scriptures:

JAMES 4:7— *Submit yourselves, then, to God. Resist the devil, and he will flee from you.*

JOHN 10:10— *The thief comes only to steal and kill and destroy; I have come that they may have life, and have it to the fullest.*

ROMANS 12:2— *Do not be conformed to this world and age, which is fashioned after and adapted to its external, superficial customs, but be transformed and changed by the entire renewal of your mind by its new ideals and its new attitude, so that you may prove for yourselves what is the good and acceptable and perfect will of God, even the thing which is good and acceptable and perfect in His sight for you.*

1 PETER 3:3-4— *Don't be concerned about the outward beauty of fancy hairstyles, expensive jewelry, or beautiful clothes. You should clothe yourselves instead with the beauty that comes from within, the unfading beauty of a gentle and quiet spirit, which is so precious to God.*

TITUS 2:12— *The Word teaches us to say "No" to ungodliness and worldly passions, and to live self-controlled, upright and godly lives in this present age.*

1 CORINTHIANS 6:19-20— *Do you not know that your body is a temple of the Holy Spirit, who is in you, whom you have received from God? You are not your own; you were bought at a price. Therefore honor God with your body.*

1 PETER 5:8— *Be self-controlled and alert. Your enemy the devil prowls around like a roaring lion looking for someone to devour.*

1 TIMOTHY 4:12— *Don't let anyone look down on you because you are young, but set an example for the believers in speech, in life, in love, in faith and in purity.*

1 TIMOTHY 5:1-2— *Do not rebuke an older man harshly, but exhort him as if he were your father. Treat younger men as brothers, older women as mothers, and younger women as sisters, with absolute purity.*

1 CORINTHIANS 10:13— *No temptation has seized you except what is common to man. And God is faithful; he will not let you be tempted beyond what you can bear. But when you are tempted, he will also provide a way out so that you can stand up under it.*

EPHESIANS 4:22-24— *You were taught, with regard to your former way of life, to put off your old self, which is being corrupted by its deceitful desires; to be made new in the attitude of your minds; and to put on the new self, created to be like God in true righteousness and holiness.*

Scripture to Memorize

I SAMUEL 16:7— *The Lord does not look at the things man looks at. Man looks at the outward appearance, but the Lord looks at the heart.*

Chapter 4
THE PASSIONATE PURSUIT
FOR INDEPENENCE

I OFTEN DAYDREAMED ABOUT BEING ABLE TO LIVE ON MY OWN and be self-sufficient. As a "free spirit," I was growing weary of living at home where everyone told me what to do... especially parents and teachers. I couldn't wait to get a job, buy a car, and move out on my own.

The "package of independence" I was looking for would certainly contain a great moneymaking job in the "real" world and my own apartment. My heart leaped at the thought of having my own space. So I started interviewing for jobs in St. Louis.

There were lots of available jobs, but finding one I *liked* was a whole other challenge. Flipping burgers at the bowling alley snack bar lost its appeal after about three weeks. The *characters* that stood at the end of the counter became the most interesting part of the job. I was the sounding board for every lonely and troubled bowler needing to talk. The constant stream of human crises soon wore me out. And reeking of cigarette smoke and grease at the end of the day was not my idea of a glamorous job. I was in the wrong business, trying to be a "shrink" for those tormented souls.

Following that, I worked in airport security and as a customer service representative for a manufacturer. Those jobs were still not what I was looking for either.

Although I had a great relationship with my parents, I really wanted to be on my own. I wanted to be a "grown up" and make decisions for myself, to experience life on my own terms.

Digging through the possibilities, I tried to define my career goals. I wanted to see the world with a job that was flexible, challenging, daring, and prosperous. Over the next few days, I narrowed the options and decided to be a flight attendant.

Our house was not quite a mile from the airport, so at night I laid in bed listening to the distant rumbling of jet engines. That was the sound of freedom. Finally, I had sufficient purpose and motivation to start running several miles everyday. My track of sidewalks took me along the edge of the airport and back. At the high point of the course, I could see the great steel birds take flight and smell the jet fumes. Somehow it fueled my determination to work out a little harder. At times the intense longing turned into tears as I prayed, "Lord, I want to be a flight attendant on one of those airlines so badly. I want to go to the ends of the earth to explore and experience other cultures…. and please Lord, could You make it happen sooner rather than later?" It wasn't long before my target weight was in clear view and it was time to apply for my dream job.

I didn't have to wait long. Within a few months, I received a letter from American Airlines to schedule an interview, which turned out to be a breeze. Then came the letter of acceptance. Soon, I flew to Dallas to begin the five-week training course.

The training was more stressful than I ever imagined. In addition to textbook study, we had frequent weigh-ins and appearance overviews where make-up had to be "pleasingly applied" and every hair in place. That part reminded me of the Barbizon days.

At the training center, a bad day could produce a "going home" slip. The silent filtering process discouraged us from making friends. A new friend could be the next one to disappear from the campus. At the end of the day, when we returned to our dorms, we often found more empty beds and cleaned out lockers. The dismissal phantom had struck again. We dared not cry or complain because it seemed that even the walls had ears.

In the middle of the five-week training period I remembered we had family friends who lived in Dallas. Since I was a little lonely, I called to see if I could go to church with them. They were delighted to hear from me and agreed to pick me up Sunday morning. Upon arrival at the church, we slipped into the last row. It felt good to be back in church again.

After the service, my friends introduced me to the pastor and his wife. They were a handsome couple. Fireworks went off inside as I shook the pastor's hand. He was the most striking man I had ever laid eyes on. His thick dark hair framed and magnified his piercing blue eyes. His captivating gaze seemed to call me to forbidden waters. I quickly looked away. I thought, *what is wrong with me? This man's wife is standing right next to him.* I knew that if I didn't leave immediately, my countenance would give away the secret attraction stirring in my heart.

Later, my friends told me that the pastor used to fly for American Airlines. They further explained, "That's why he loves to talk to people going through training. He enjoyed being a flight attendant, but had to give it up for full time ministry." They also told me he was a part time model in Dallas. So, that explained it! I had been attracted to him because he was so incredibly handsome. It was nothing more, so I dismissed the encounter.

Several days later, at the training center, I was told I had a personal phone call waiting. I was shocked when I picked up the phone and heard the pastor's voice. He said he was just checking on me because he knew how intense the weeks of training could be. Then added, "I got your information from the visitor card you filled out on Sunday. I hope it's OK that I called you." Frankly, I was relieved to have someone to talk to, so we chatted for a while. He said he might stop by to see me in a day or two and say "hello" to his friends who were still working there.

He showed up Friday afternoon. After talking to some of his friends, he turned to me with a suggestion that took me by surprise. "Would you like to get out of here for a little while?" he asked. "Why don't we go get something to eat?" Of course, questions raced through my mind. According to my upbringing, a married pastor was not supposed to go out with a single girl. But, maybe I was wrong. Maybe it was just a cultural issue, approved in Texas but not where I grew up.

As the night grew late, it became clear that his intentions were not pure. He showered me with affection and whispered his predatory desires. I was caught in a swirling vortex of confusion, naïveté, danger, and his magnetic charisma. After much persistence, I finally surrendered to him.

Our silent ride back to the training center was followed by a cold "good night." I had just been seduced and duped by someone I trusted to be safe. Of course, that trust was assumed by his role as a pastor! How could he stand in the pulpit on Sunday, preaching the Word of God, and then turn right around and be completely godless. I felt like I had just been in the presence of "Dr. Jekyll and Mr. Hyde."

I wanted to scream the injustice of it and expose the wrong I had just experienced, but there was no one in the dorm I could trust. And no one would have cared. I quietly slid into bed. My heart felt cold and abandoned. Not even the blankets brought warmth. I finally fell asleep in silent disgrace.

The last day of training came as we weighed in. The clang of metal weights slid across the balance bar, and miraculously landed within the "hiring weight" range. The battle of the bulge was defeated one more time. The entire five-week training had been one continual emotional test, which made passing the written exams easy. Breathing a huge sigh of relief to have finished the course, I headed down the hall for my last interview.

Sitting across the desk was a well-dressed, white haired gentleman. The deep graceful wrinkles on his face reflected his many years as a vice-president of American Airlines. He asked me to be seated. Then, he asked questions that would determine my ability to be a successful flight attendant. His last question was, "What is your primary responsibility as a flight attendant?" I spoke one word: "Safety." He beamed, "Yes! That's exactly right. Welcome to American Airlines."

I had never heard such beautiful words! As I shook his hand, I thanked him and then raced out the door.

One final decision needed to be made. Where did I want to live? Each flight attendant bid on one of the five base cities. I quickly put New York City at the top of my list. Why? Because it was the biggest and most terrifying city and I wanted to conquer the fear of it. When the bids were handed out, guess what city I got? New York! I was so happy and scared at the same time. Moving there seemed like the perfect challenge for me.

Crazy parties celebrated those who had passed the grueling weeks of training. Everyone had been in the same pressure cooker; we were all happy to release the stress valve. At one of those parties, my friend Tami and I met Shane, another flight attendant who had just rented an apartment on Long Island. He said we were welcome to stay with him until we found our own place.

Back in St. Louis I packed the car. I thought leaving home would be easy. After all, I was finally on my way, establishing my independence. But driving away, looking at mom and dad in the rearview mirror, I couldn't fight back the tears. I knew my world would never be the same again.

After hours of driving, weariness and fatigue began to set in. The earlier excitement faded as the magnitude of my new reality hit. Courage shrank into the shadows as fear became my new companion. Running my fingers through my hair, I leaned back against the seat and muttered, "Was I crazy to choose New York City?" How would I ever survive a new job, a new city, and working out of three different airports, with no family nearby, no church, no place to call home? I sobbed, "Oh my God, what have I done?"

Fifteen hours later, I arrived at Shane's apartment. He and Tami greeted me with hugs. Over the next six weeks, Tami and I lived crammed into a tiny bedroom. All our boxed belongings were piled to the ceiling around our mattress on the floor.

Naturally, we were desperate to find our own apartment.

After realizing that Manhattan was so loud, cramped, and expensive, we broadened our search and landed in the small community of Great Neck, New York. A little elderly lady was renting a flat on the second floor of her residential home. We met her, looked at the rooms and immediately fell in love with it. It was exactly what we wanted. Opening the door with my new key, I raced up the steps to my very own bedroom. The birds were singing. A gentle wind blew through the open windows. The drapes floated on the wind, like welcoming arms. I ran to look outside my window and there it was… something other than a paved surface—a green manicured lawn. I was so grateful. Carrying in the last box from the car, I closed the door behind me to pause in a moment of gratitude. "Thank you Lord, for our new refuge, away from the noise and clatter of the city."

Soon Tami and I were flying opposite schedules so I only saw her about once a month. Most of the rookies, like me, were on reserve so we rarely flew with any of our friends. Weeks would slip by without a single interaction with anyone I knew. Soon, my isolation and loneliness turned to depression. What I thought would be the pinnacle of freedom was turning into the opposite. Commuting through the concrete jungle of high-rise buildings, and running through airports...it all began to feel like a prison.

Desperate for friendship, I visited several churches. Every one of them seemed wacky. I didn't know which was worse, the screaming preachers, political speeches, or the cold and impersonal responses of those who sat next to me in the pew. Since that didn't seem to be working, I turned to plan B. The television show, "Cheers," always painted a friendly atmosphere for those who hung out at their local bar. It was "where everybody knows your name." So I thought I would give it a try.

One day, driving by the quaint shops of downtown Great Neck, I found a cozy restaurant and bar just a few blocks from our flat. As I walked through the door, I quickly became aware that I was one of the few Gentiles in the place. All heads turned with curiosity. My fair skin and green eyes were a dead give away that I wasn't from around there. After a few stiff drinks, nestled at the bar, it didn't really matter anymore and with each sip, the heartache of loneliness subsided.

I began to frequent their happy hour and it wasn't long before I made friends. I met a Jewish guy who must have needed a friend too. As weeks went by, we started hanging out together. Oddly enough, I wasn't at all attracted to him, but he was kind to me and I so desperately needed a friend. Ira was an influential man. Even though I liked him, he carried a shadow of treachery I didn't trust. I was grateful for his companionship and generosity as he wined and dined me but I kept my heart guarded. He was not the marrying type and certainly not a man I could fall in love with.

He socialized with the upper class and started taking me to private parties. His friends owned huge estates in the Hamptons. It wasn't long before I discovered that many of them were wealthy Mafia leaders. Their lives intrigued me. It was like living in a scene from," The Godfather." But these guys were real characters, not actors.

I was amazed to see how wealth had affected them. It hadn't revealed—or given them—any significant purpose in life. They were exquisitely dressed and draped with jewels, but their lost souls were aimlessly drifting through life, just waiting for the pleasure of another party. I realized how much those people *really* needed Jesus. And, all the while, I was drifting farther and farther away from Him myself.

One day, during an incredible heat wave, I thought I was going to die from the heat. So, in desperation, I called Ira. He invited me to come over to his air-conditioned place. I jumped in the car and drove a short distance to his apartment. I was so happy to have a cool place for the afternoon.

As I entered Ira's kitchen, he was sitting at the table, which was covered with a white powder. He was using a razor blade to build small ridges of powder and carefully scooping each one into separate plastic bags. As I drew closer, a cold shiver ran down my spine. Could this be? "Surely that isn't what I think it is!" I said in horror. He licked his fingers and proudly said, "Yes. This is the best cocaine I have ever had!"

"Oh my God," I said, "You're a dealer!"

"And what is wrong with that?" he indignantly replied. The realization of his "real" job and the dangerous company I had gotten involved with scared me to death.

Within a few minutes, I walked out the door. I don't even remember saying goodbye. I was back in the heat but it didn't matter anymore. My mind was made up; I couldn't stay there, not for one more minute, heat wave or no heat wave. What had I gotten myself into? I was running with drug dealers and Mafia leaders. I had innocently become wrapped in a web of danger. I had to get out of there!

I began spending most of my time off at Long Island Beach. At least it was cooler in the ocean breezes. Ira left peace offerings and "I'm sorry" notes on the steps of my flat, but nothing would change my mind. I knew I couldn't see him again. In my weakened spiritual state, I wasn't strong enough to be a positive influence in his life. And at that point, his lifestyle was dragging me down a dark and treacherous road.

Then one day, good news came. I had finished the three months probation with the airline. That entitled me to a free ticket anywhere I wanted to go. I just wanted to go home where it was safe. I wanted to be close to mom and dad.

I didn't tell them I was coming. Upon arriving at the St. Louis airport, I took a taxi to their house. I stepped up to the front door and rang the doorbell as if I was a stranger. When my mother opened the door she said, "Yes… may I help you?" In disbelief, I said, "Mom, it's me!" She gasped with surprise, "Honey, what are you doing here? Well…you don't even look like yourself!" Her comment struck me to the core. I didn't realize how much I had changed. I think I knew that months of loneliness, stress and distance from God had hardened my heart. But until that moment I didn't realized how it had changed my countenance! I had become as tough and hard as the concrete runways we landed on.

Three months later I received notice that American was laying off fifteen hundred flight attendants. I immediately called Operations; they confirmed that my name was on the list of those being furloughed. As I hung up the phone, I cried for joy. Never before had I been so ecstatic about losing a job.

I had no reason to stay in New York; I was going home! I had no idea what I would do, but anything was better than the life I was living. My vitality had been eroded by loneliness and isolation. It felt like the fire of my soul had gone out.

Glancing at the New York City skyline in my rear view mirror, I thought about the prodigal son. He didn't *deserve* any favors from his father but anything was better than what he had. Likewise, I knew the Lord didn't owe me anything, but I wanted to make things right! I had to go home. We had a grand reunion as I arrived at my parent's home.

The following weekend, my parents invited me to go with them to a new church called Grace World Outreach Church. Strangely numb and disconnected, I agreed to go. From the first song the Spirit of God began to bathe my soul with His love. As I "soaked" in worship, my spirit stirred for the first time in a long time. Overwhelmed by my emptiness, I cried and cried and cried until I couldn't cry anymore. The Father had embraced His prodigal daughter. Through traveling the hard road I discovered my greatest need was not *independence* from—but *dependence* on—the Lord.

Week Four   [Date: _____]

Pick one day out of your week when you can take time to sit and reflect on the following thoughts and respond to the meditation questions below.

Fourth Key To Becoming Free: *Submit Your Passionate Pursuits to the Lord.*

I wanted to be in charge of my life so I took matters into my own hands. I was determined to do things "my way." I knew what I wanted and I went after it. I didn't want to ask for anyone's help, including God. I felt I could handle my life just fine.

There is nothing wrong with pursuing one's passions. The issue is how it is done. I was like a sheep gone astray, pursuing my passions without consulting the Lord. *All we like sheep have gone astray; we have turned—every one—to his own way* —Isaiah 53:6[20]

Doing anything I wanted to do didn't bring happiness. And, worse, living apart from the Lord was toxic. Being in the center of His will was the only way to find true fulfillment and happiness. I learned it the hard way. The lessons I learned removed the illusions of self-reliance and the need to prove myself. At last, I found rest in Him as I put Him in charge of my life. He was far more capable of taking care of me than I was.

Nuggets of Truth

God knows us better than we know ourselves. He intricately formed our DNA in our mother's womb, so He knows what makes us happy and what makes us sad.

Many times, while trying to achieve happiness and fulfillment, we loose sight of the only One who can give it. Even when we make wrong choices, He is the Redeemer of ALL things; there is no such thing as a permanent mistake in life. God promises to use *everything* for our good. Those choices may cause us to take the long way around to get back to Him but He uses that journe￼ to humble us, soften our heart and strengthen our trust in H'

As I look back, there was one other thing I needed to settle. Through my search for independence, I also wanted to prove the validity of Christianity. I had been taught to live a Christian life, but something inside me wasn't convinced. I honestly wondered if it really mattered, so I set out to find the answer. I soon found out that life outside of a passionate relationship with Jesus Christ is empty.

So my advice is simply this: Don't waste years of your life looking for happiness in anything else. If you are one who thrives on adventure like me, let Jesus take you on adventures that will live forever. Instead of disappointment, His unforgettable journeys will provide you with lasting joy, fulfillment and reward. As you grow older, every time you recall them, they will be life to you.

Meditation Questions

Take time to examine your heart and true feelings and then write them down. It will help you understand who you are and what you want in life. Then ask the Lord to mature, within you, His design and calling.

1. What are some unfulfilled passions in your life?

   _____

   _____

   _____

   _____

2. Are those passions in alignment with the word of God? It's important to make sure your passions are not opposing a healthy relationship with the lord.

   _____

   _____

3. What is standing in your way of achieving them? Are you feeling limited by ability, energy, time, resources,

others, etc.? (name them) Remember that nothing is impossible with God.

_____

_____

_____

_____

4. What steps do you need to take to achieve your goals? Write them down and begin to work toward your goal one day at a time. Many times the Lord expects us to take the first step and He meets us there.

_____

_____

_____

_____

Prayer

As you read this prayer, make it your own.

> *Father, I ask that You reveal the true passions of my heart. I want to discover and pursue the ones You intended for me to go after, the ones You wove into my DNA as I was formed...not the ones that I may have fabricated out of my own selfish ambition. You created me as a very special person, unique in every way. I am an original, not a copy of any other person. Therefore, I know there are extraordinary opportunities and friendships that are designed specifically for me, ones that will bring great joy and fulfillment.*
>
> *Today, I'm asking You to place me on the track of Your divine purposes and redeem any wrong choices I have made.*

> Your Word says that all things work for the good of those who trust in You. So today, I am placing my trust in You. Holy Spirit, prompt me to choose rightly and bring me to new seasons of adventure, learning and growing which lead to lasting happiness and fulfillment. I thank You for who You are and what You are doing in my life. In Jesus' Name, Amen.

Additional Scripture References

Take time to read these scriptures. They will strengthen you as you are reminded of His promises to you.

PSALM 34:22— *The LORD redeems his servants; no one will be condemned who takes refuge in him.*

PSALM 84:11— *For the LORD God is a sun and shield; the LORD bestows favor and honor; no good thing does he withhold from those whose walk is blameless.*

DEUTERONOMY 8:7— *For the LORD your God is bringing you into a good land—a land with streams and pools of water, with springs flowing in the valleys and hills.*

PSALM 139:13-15— *For you created my inmost being; you knit me together in my mother's womb. I praise you because I am fearfully and wonderfully made; your works are wonderful, I know that full well.*

ROMANS 8:28— *And we know that in all things God works for the good of those who love him, who have been called according to his purpose.*

Scripture to Memorize

JEREMIAH 29:11— *For I know the plans I have for you, declares the LORD, plans to prosper you and not to harm you, plans to give you hope and a future.*

Endnotes

[20]Scripture quotation from The Holy Bible, English Standard Version® (ESV®), copyright © 2001 by Crossway, a publishing ministry of Good News Publishers. Used by permission. All rights reserved."

Chapter 5

FINDING TRUE LOVE

LIKE MOST LITTLE GIRLS, I FANTASIZED ABOUT BEING CINDERELLA and being swept away by a handsome prince who lived in a beautiful castle.

I started dreaming about it in the second grade. In the first few weeks of Mrs. Harp's class, I sat in the back of the room to check out all of the boys. It wasn't long before I selected a boy who I deemed worthy of my attention. Without knowing it, he passed my juvenile tests. But, at seven years old, my requirements weren't very complicated. The winner would have dark hair, be nice, and smile at me often. And, oh yeah, he couldn't be stinky.

The next year, I had two boyfriends. Whoever was friendlier to me, on any given day, was my favorite. Zoning in and out of math class, I would practice writing my first name followed by their last name, trying to decide which one looked and sounded better if we got married.

Since our family didn't live in town, I rarely saw my classmates over the summers. So when school started again in the fall, it was like having all new boyfriend possibilities. In fact, throughout the year, it was not unusual for me to fall in and out of "love" several times a week.

I knew I wasn't cute and feminine like the other girls. I was a tomboy. In sixth grade, I was not only growing up but I was also growing out. It was probably those two or three Carmello candy bars I ate every day from the snack bar. Plus the extra milk and cookies that others didn't want at lunchtime. But an amazing thing happened the summer after eighth-grade graduation. When all the hormones kicked into overdrive, my "barrel" figure suddenly changed to voluptuous curves as I grew tall and thin. My personality changed too. I had been an introvert, but that shy person stepped away as "Cinderella" stepped out, ready to meet her handsome prince.

In the ninth grade, reading romance novels from the school library consumed every waking hour. As I devoured each new story, I felt my heart race at the sensual tension mounting as two people tried to resist falling in love. Every study hall, bus ride and evening (after homework), I escaped to my world of romantic intrigue. Sometimes I read a book a day. At bedtime when dad said, "Lights out," I pulled the covers over my head, snuggled up with my feather pillow and read by flashlight. Holding the book so close, I could smell the dusty pages. I had one goal in mind as I headed for the last chapter. All the tension would be released when the couple kissed followed by the words, "And they lived happily ever after. The End." Then I closed the book, turned off the flashlight and drifted into sleep where I could become the one who has just been rescued by love.

Every time I saw the movie "Cinderella," I sat spellbound and cried as if it was the first time all over again. When the glass slipper fit, their search for belonging and years of agonizing loneliness were finally over. They were so beautiful together. She was the fair maiden and he was dark and mysterious, just like the man I hoped to find someday.

Suitors started asking dad for my hand in marriage as soon as I turned 14. Finding someone that wanted to marry me was not the problem. Finding someone I wanted to marry was a whole other story.

The man who would win my heart had to love adventure, be brave but gentle, and have strength of character. He had to be true and loyal, not only to me but to God. I knew I was a handful of independence, so he had to be a secure man. He must be humored by my silliness and not threatened by my intensity. Of course, all the normal stuff was on the list too, such as: tall, dark and handsome. Oh yeah.... and rich too. In fact, my list was two pages long! I knew it was a lot to ask for but I was certain he was out there.

Over the next ten years, dating became one of my favorite pastimes. I broke a few hearts and a few broke mine while sailing in and out of relationships. Three different times I agreed to marry someone, but the Lord intervened to make it clear the match was not "made in heaven." In my desperation to find a soul mate, I kissed a lot of "ugly toads" along the way. Well, they weren't exactly ugly; 1 always prided myself for dating "lookers." But, I knew if they were missing the right values, and if the inside beauty didn't match the outside, we would never truly be happy together.

Unfortunately, there were a couple of times when character flaws didn't surface until the relationship had gone on too long, even to the point of engagement. When I finally saw the warning signs, I denied them because I had grown comfortable and fond of that person. So instead of ending the relationship, I coasted along, caught up in the security of "belonging" to someone instead of seriously considering what that commitment might demand later.

Many saw my desperation to find "the one" and tried to help me. I had several well-meaning friends who played the matchmaker game. It always amazed me what kind of guy they thought I would like; blind dates were the worst!

I still had flashbacks of "Ichabod Crane" who escorted me to dinner and the theater one evening. When the doorbell rang on that cold rainy night in October, I opened the door and couldn't believe what I saw. Under a dark and dripping trench coat stood a very tall, gangly man. Greasy tresses of hair protruded from his top hat. His face was pasty white and his sharp crooked nose overshadowed all other facial features. Even the heavy presence of cologne could not camouflage the lack of hygiene. I expected someone to yell, "Smile, you're on Candid Camera!!" But, no one did.

As we walked to the car, Ichabod held the umbrella over himself while I walked in the rain. At dinner, he asked if we could split an entrée and insisted I pay for my half! When we arrived at the theater, he parked in a mud puddle that covered my strapped heels as I stepped out of the car.

At intermission, he purchased one gigantic coke from the concession stand; he thought I wouldn't mind sharing it with him. When the intermission ended, Ichabod parked his trashcan-sized drink behind a potted plant in the foyer, saying, "Since we can't take drinks into the theater, I'll finish it when we come out." But, by that point, he had consumed so much coke that, during the second half of the play, he had to go to the bathroom numerous times. He had to climb over an entire row of people to get to the aisle. It was like the old Bugs Bunny cartoon—"Excuse me, pardon me, excuse me, pardon me"—all the way to the aisle. I was mortified! I was never so relieved when we finally pulled up in front of our house. My skin crawled as I slammed the car door behind me. Breathing a sigh of relief, I vowed never go on a blind date again!

One day, a friend said, " Leann, there is a drummer named Carl Albrecht I think you should meet. There's something special about him." Honestly, I wasn't at all interested in a musician or a blind date so I nonchalantly replied; "Maybe I can meet him over coffee sometime." I had no idea how prophetic that statement would become.

Months later, during a lead vocal session, we took a break because I was in desperate need of a caffeine boost. When I reached the coffee machine in the lounge, my heart sank as I picked up an empty pot. I didn't have a clue how to make more coffee. I turned around to see a blond stranger sitting at the other end of the room, intently writing music charts. Hesitant to interrupt him, I politely asked, "Excuse me, do you have any idea how to use this machine?" He looked up and said, "Yes, of course. We have one similar to that at our house." Soon, the smell of fresh brewing coffee filled the air as the dark liquid drug began to drip. Caffeine was on its way!

While we stood there waiting for the coffee to brew, I said, "My name is Leann Hendrickson," and extended my hand to greet him.

"Oh hi, my name is Carl Albrecht." We looked at each other in disbelief! Following an awkward moment of realization, we both said, simultaneously, "So you're the one I've heard about."

I'm not sure what was going on in his mind at that moment, but I was already drawing definite conclusions of my own. Sure, he was nice, but I certainly couldn't see what everybody was raving about. I wouldn't see or think about Carl again for a long time.

Two years later, my boyfriend Bill and I decided to take thirty days apart from each other to seek the Lord regarding our relationship. He wanted to get married, but I needed more time. During that week, the name, "Carl Albrecht" kept coming to my mind. The memory of our meeting was vague and unimpressive so I called my friend, Corin, who knew him. "Don't you know a drummer named Carl Albrecht? I asked. "Where is he and what is he doing nowadays?" She replied, "Oh sure. In fact, he is playing for a band called 'September' and they are playing this weekend in downtown St. Louis at the VP Fair."

I said, "See if you can find out their schedule and maybe we can go see them play." I was relieved that she didn't ask any questions. She already knew I had been unhappy with Bill for some time. Within an hour we were on our way downtown.

We found "September" and listened to the show. When they finished the set, Carl spotted Corin in the crowd and made a bee-line to greet her. As he got closer, he saw me standing there too. I could tell by the look on his face he was shocked but pleasantly surprised. When he finished hugging Corin, he threw his arms around me as if I was a long-lost friend. He seemed different from the first time I met him. He carried a confidence and manliness that attracted me.

Making our way back to the car, I told Corin I was profoundly impacted by Carl's ability to play drums. Like most people, I had never given drums much thought. But, each note Carl played resounded with accuracy, peace, and stability. I literally felt safe

and calm within the beat of his drums. Corin said, "They're playing again tomorrow on the main stage under the Arch. Do you
want to go?"

"Absolutely."

The next afternoon Corin and I made our way to the stage to say
hello. Carl looked up and our eyes met. Once again he came to the
side of the stage to greet us. He looked even better in daylight as
the wind caught his silky blond hair, highlighting his suntanned
face. His dimples were boyish and innocent, but his countenance
was that of man.

When the concert started we found a place to sit on the grassy
hillside. I was quickly drawn into the music. The band was fabu-
lous but my eyes were fixed on Carl. It was as though I was getting
to know him with every poetic rhythm. Not wanting to disclose
my attraction to him, Corin and I once again vanished before the
concert was over.

Two days later, my phone rang. It was Carl! "Hi, Leann. I hope
you don't mind, but I got your number from John." It felt like destiny was unfolding at that moment because the Lord had answered
my prayer. I had made myself available for Carl by showing up
two days in a row to hear him play. I needed to know it was a "God
thing" by asking the Lord for Carl to make the next move. After
a few minutes of chitchat, my heart fluttered as he said, "Would
you like to go out to dinner with me sometime?" By the end of the
conversation, we had planned a date.

The following Saturday, he picked me up in his pale yellow
Pinto station wagon. Sitting next to him, I was a little surprised
by his demeanor. Although he seemed like such a monster personality when he played drums, Carl was thoughtful, gentle and
easy going. Early in the afternoon I could feel myself relaxing and
I felt safe when I was around him. After an early dinner at T.G.I.
Friday's, the date continued. The evening light was dazzling as we
strolled beside a nearby lake. Along the path, Carl reached over
to hold my hand, which took me by surprise. I thought that was a

little forward for the first date. Even though I felt awkward, I continued to let him hold it as we walked back to the car.

It was too early to go home so we stopped at another street festival to hear some jazz. It was at that moment we discovered that although we appreciate all kinds of music, jazz was definitely the sound that soothed our souls. As he walked me to the door that evening, he said, "I would like to see you again sometime." I heard myself say, "How about tomorrow?" He quickly agreed.

The next day, a sweltering summer Saturday, we headed for a picnic in a town nearby where the Albrecht family band was performing. Carl thought it would be the perfect opportunity for me to meet them. They had just taken a break when Carl introduced me to them. I was taken off guard with how little acknowledgement they gave to either one of us. I began to think the worst. By the end of the day, I concluded a relationship with Carl would never work because I didn't fit with his family. Even though I had grown fond of Carl, I needed to stop seeing him immediately. If I waited, it would just get harder. I had no intention of seeing him again as we said goodbye that night.

But, as we were parting, he turned to me and said, "I love you." His steady gaze spoke a thousand words in three and I knew he meant them. Under normal circumstances, that little phrase is what a person longs for and waits to hear. However, still feeling the fresh defeat of meeting his family and the fact we had only known each other for two days, I thought the man had lost his mind! I was speechless. All I could do was give him a quick hug before he left. When I closed the door, I figured it was over. My heart was torn and sad. I really liked him, but I was convinced there was no chance it could work.

The following week, my parents and I flew out to visit my aunt in Seattle. I was relieved to get away from St. Louis so I wouldn't have to answer Carl's calls....*if* he called. Sitting on the plane, looking out the window, I was terribly confused as I replayed the events of the weekend. I sorted through all the mixed signals—

from God, from Carl's family, from my own heart. I was truly perplexed. Slowly, my thoughts drifted back to Bill who was patiently
waiting for me to make a decision concerning our marriage. We
had not spoken to each other for several weeks.

Bill was a great Christian guy and everyone seemed to like him.
He was so affectionate and spontaneous which was very attractive
to my "gypsy" attitude about life. However, as much as I tried, I
couldn't seem to get my heart settled on "being in love" with him.
But, I sure loved his family. They treated me like a daughter, and
his sisters became the ones I never had. Even though Bill and I
fought constantly, I thought it must be the devil trying to keep us
apart. If we got married, I hoped it would get better and I would
fall in love with him somewhere along the line. I was sure I could
change him after we said our, "I do's."

While I was still in Seattle, Bill and I had a tender phone conversation in which I agreed to marry him. As soon as I returned
to St. Louis, we would make an official announcement. But, soon
after I returned home, the fighting started up again. Again, I was
so perplexed! Why couldn't we get along? I was desperate for an
answer from God to know what was wrong with our relationship.

Our church was planning a huge event and asked me to be one
of the featured artists. As it turned out, Carl was recruited to play
drums in my band. The rehearsal was the first time we had seen
each other in nearly two months. During a break, Carl ran into a
friend who blurted out, "Hey, Carl. Have you heard the good news?
Leann is getting married!" Stunned, Carl responded hesitantly,
"No…no, I hadn't heard about that." As soon as the rehearsal was
over that evening, Carl walked straight up to me. Sternly, he said,
"I want to talk to you! Come over here and sit down with me." As
we sat down I could see his troubled countenance, "I just heard
that you are going to marry Bill!" Then looking intently into my
eyes he asked, "Are you sure you want to do that?"

Taken off guard by his intrusive question, I responded indignantly, "Yes, I know what I'm doing. I am sure this is what I want

to do!" But, during the rest of the weekend, Carl's words—"Are you sure?"—kept haunting me. I *wasn't* sure.

As a flight attendant, I resumed my schedule that next week. Several years had passed since I was a flight attendant with American Airlines. I still loved flying so I started working with a new airline called Air One. Somewhere between St. Louis and New York, standing in front of the ovens, I heard an audible voice say, "No!" It was so loud I spun around to see who had spoken to me. There wasn't a soul in sight. Suddenly, I recalled the story of God speaking audibly to Samuel. That sent a shiver down my spine; I replied, "Yes, Lord… what is it?" Then He spoke gently to my spirit and said, "Bill is not the one for you. I have someone who is better suited for him and I have someone better suited for you." That's all He said. It was over; my question was firmly answered. It felt like a warm blanket had just been wrapped around my heart. All the anguish and confusion left.

By the time the plane landed, the Lord had completely severed that relationship. It was as though we had never dated. When we landed, I called Bill. As I told him what the Lord said, he seemed disappointed, but not devastated…much to my relief.

Obviously, after clearly hearing the voice of the Lord, everything changed inside me. I was no longer anxious about finding a husband. For the first time, I knew I would rather be single the rest of my life than be married to the wrong person. I had failed miserably at finding the "perfect man" in my own strength and understanding. At that point, I was relieved that the "pursuit" was over. Now I could turn all my attention and affection toward the Lord. Since He said he had someone for me, *He* could bring him into my life. *I* was going to stop looking. A deep contentment settled over me as I let go of the quest to be married. The struggle was over.

The big celebration finally arrived. I was excited about the concert, but I was reluctant to see Carl again. As I greeted the band, Carl asked, "How are the wedding plans coming along?" I quickly replied, "They're fine." I was not about to tell him or anyone else, I had just broken off my engagement with Bill! I already felt like such a "flake head" about the whole ordeal, I didn't need that opinion reinforced!

After the concert, Carl and several people decided to go to a Denny's Restaurant. I was so hungry, I couldn't wait for the first bite of a steaming hot Western omelet filled with bell peppers, green onions, and dripping with cheese.

While leaving, Carl offered to take me back to my car at the church parking lot. As we drove, he asked me how the wedding was coming along. I had to tell the truth, so looking away I said, "I'm not engaged to Bill anymore." And I told him all the agonizing details that had transpired the last few days, including what the Lord spoke to me on the airplane.

After talking about various relationship issues, Carl asked, "What are you looking for in a husband? How many children do you want?" From there, we volleyed for hours with more questions like:

"What are your goals in life and what do you see yourself doing in ten years?

"How much money do you make and how much debt do you have?"

"Does it matter if your spouse makes more money than you do?"

"After you get married, how often do you want sex?" Carl laughingly responded, "Every day, of course." We covered doctrinal issues, family values and told our stories of how we got saved. There was no topic unturned.

All of a sudden, a shift took place. Without planning it, it seemed we were interviewing each other for marriage. As the night wore on, a veil lifted from my eyes and I saw Carl differently. Because there had been no pretense we were able to ask questions and give answers without fear of rejection. Every answer he gave completely aligned with the secret desires of my heart for a husband. Silence fell as our seamless conversation came to an end. The question vault was empty. Like an old married couple, we sat there completely comfortable in each other's company. Stress and tension was gone and any bubble of mystery had been burst as we sufficiently drew out the truth from each other's heart.

It was 4:00 A.M.!

That week, Carl left on tour with his band and he said he would call me from the road. While he was gone, I went to see an old friend who had a prophetic gift. I told her all the details of the break-up with Bill and meeting Carl. She said, "Leann, I feel like the man you will marry is *waiting in the wings*." Later that night Carl called. As we talked, out of the blue he said, "Leann, I just feel like I am *waiting in the wings*...waiting to come on stage." I dropped the phone and ran to the other side of the apartment to scream and dance a jig! There was no way he could have known the prophetic word just spoken to me! When I went back and picked up the phone, he said, "Are you OK?" I assured him I was and changed the subject as quickly as I could. I wanted the Lord to be the One Who revealed His plan for us, not me.

Our times together were so different from other relationships. It felt more like we were preparing for marriage instead of dating. There was so much peace between us. I couldn't wait to see him as often as I could.

One day, a few months later, I had a meltdown and accused him of not loving me. He came over and put my face in his hands and emphatically said, "Leann, I wouldn't have married you, if I didn't love you!" Suddenly, we both pulled away and froze, stunned by what he just said. "Well...," he said, "I guess, in my heart it feels like I am already married to you.... so..." he paused to take a breath, then looking deep into my eyes he said, "Will you marry me?" All the floodgates of emotion burst open. Through my tears of joy, I gave a soggy, "yes." He wrapped his arms around me. I continued to cry as I buried my face in his chest.

Six months later we were married. God led me to my handsome prince. Our love has deepened through the years. He has not only been my husband, but my friend and soul mate. We will live... happily ever after.

Week Five   [Date: _____]

Pick one day out of your week when you can take time to sit and reflect on the following thoughts and respond to the meditation questions below.

Fifth Step in Becoming Free: *Allow the Lord to complete His Perfect Love in you.*

I spent many years looking for true love…from the second grade until I was twenty-seven years old. I tried to find someone who completed my longing for love instead of looking to the Lord for that fulfillment.

What would I have done differently? I would have spent more time investing in my relationship with the Lord, family and friends. I would have learned how to love others instead of waiting to pour all of it on one guy.

I would have also continued my education. I didn't allow my interests to deepen and flourish. I only had one thing on my mind…. finding a husband.

I am also keenly aware of and thankful that God restores all things and redeems wasted portions of our life. Because of His grace, mercy, and His great love that covers my mistakes, I can rest knowing His purposes and plans for my life are and will be completely fulfilled.

The attraction to the opposite sex is perfectly natural; God made us that way. It is totally normal for a woman to want a husband and a man to want a wife. The fact is, God created us to love and be loved. Love is one of the things that makes life worth living. Without love we die. Just like newborn babies, if they are fed but not loved, they die.

Although I didn't come from a broken home, I suffered from what most PKs (preacher's kids) suffer from—parents who were passionately devoted to the Lord and church ministry. Don't misunderstand me, they loved my brother and me very much but their love got spread so thin because it was also shared with an entire congregation. I don't fault my parents for that; they did the best they knew how.

No human love can satisfy the longing for love that God placed in us. Only He can completely occupy that space. Until I found His love, I continued to look for it in all the wrong places. I tried to fill that space with all the wrong people and things.

After we were married, I thought Carl could meet that need, but soon found out that he couldn't fill it either. I thought surely the most passionate love affair with my husband would finally complete me. It didn't. I still needed the love of the Lord, who was the true lover of my soul and I needed to become a true lover of Him. Carl loved me in many ways but only God could satisfy the core of my being with His perfect love.

So what is perfect love? The Bible clearly spells it out for us in I Corinthians 13:4-8. This is the kind of love that we were made to give and receive. It has no boundaries and includes all races, gender and age groups.

1 CORINTHIANS 13:4-8— *Love endures long and is patient and kind; love never is envious nor boils over with jealousy, it is not boastful or narcissistic, it does not display itself haughtily. It is not conceited, arrogant and inflated with pride; it is not rude or unmannerly and does not act indecent. Love does not insist on its own rights or its own way, for it is not self-seeking; it is not touchy or fretful or resentful; it takes no account of the evil done to it and it pays no attention to a suffered wrong. It does not rejoice at injustice and unrighteousness, but rejoices when right and truth prevail. Love bears up under anything and everything that comes, is ever ready to believe the best of every person, its hopes are fadeless under all circumstances, and it endures everything without weakening. Love never fails. It never becomes obsolete or comes to an end.*[21]

I still get lonely sometimes. If Carl and I have been on the road and not attending to each other because of our schedule, we have to stop and deliberately take time to reconnect. However, if after quality time with him my heart is still aching, I realize I have a greater need; I am also missing time with the lover of my soul, God. When I stop and allow Him to fill me up again, my heart is once again at peace. Do you know why we need the Lord to fill us up EVERY DAY? Because we leak!!! Life drains our cup of love and He is the only one whose supply is inexhaustible.

Nugget of Truth

Carl later confessed to me that when we first met, he had put me on the pedestal of his heart. He adored and idolized me. That wasn't healthy for either one of us. The Lord *allowed* the circumstances to fall apart, which devastated him at the beginning of our relationship. Carl said, "Even though it was painful, we would have been heading for trouble if it hadn't happened that way. There is only one person who should rightfully occupy that place in my heart. The Lord wasn't going to allow anyone else to take His place…. not even you."

Through the testing and crucible of twenty-six years of marriage, I am glad Carl's heart has been steadfast and his eyes have been fixed on the Lord. I could never have fulfilled the expectations of the One who rightfully held that place of prominence in his heart. The Lord has been the stabilizing force in our marriage.

It's important to honor, love and care for each other. You'll notice I put the word "honor" first, even before "love." There are days when we don't feel "in love." On those days, we must continue to honor each other. Honor means: To show high regard and respect; to respond with strong moral character, strength and dignity toward another person.

If you are in pursuit of a marriage partner for a lifelong commitment, ask the Lord to find that person. He knows you better than you know yourself and He knows who is best for you.

It's never too late to back out of a courtship when you know it's not right.

If you are a believing Christian, *do not marry one who is not.* 2 CORINTHIANS 6:14— *You are not the same as those who do not believe. So do not join yourselves to them. Good and bad do not belong together. Light and darkness cannot share together.* [22]

One common and painful mistake is the hope that a spouse will change in marriage. That's a chance you can't afford to take. People rarely change because of marriage. Once the honeymoon and passion subsides…. and it will, there must be a mutual core faith in God that carries you through difficult times. God must be the anchor for both of you.

Don't toy with another person's heart. Everyone needs and deserves respect. Don't "lead them on" for your own emotional (or other) reasons.

Guard your own heart and don't give it away until you have found the one you are looking for. How will you know the right one? Let the Spirit of the Lord confirm it! He will make it clear. He will cause peace to rest on your relationship; it will feel like warm oil flowing over your heart every time you are together. Wait for the peace. Even in an argument, the peace of God will keep you steady and preserve the mutual respect and honor between you and the right person. In fact, I think a healthy disagreement is necessary in the courting stage of any relationship. That's when you really find out what people are made of.

Here are some words of wisdom we have learned over the years:

1) Be the best cheerleader your spouse has ever had.

2) Sing his/her praises often.

3) Your goal must be to commit to serve and lay your life down for each other 100% every day. God will give you grace and fresh ideas on how to take care of your spouse so your love will continue to grow and deepen.

4) Stop all criticism of each other. Negativity will kill the strongest of hearts because, in essence, every time you criticize, you speak death over them. *The tongue has the power of life and death, and those who love it will eat its fruit.* —**Proverbs 18:21**

5) Ask the Lord to change your thought patterns. Begin to reflect on the Word of God and let Him fill you with hope so your words can be full of life.

If your marriage is in trouble, try to remember back to the beginning of your relationship. Re-evaluate the good things that made you fall in love with your spouse and capitalize on those reasons. Write them down and begin to take steps to pursue him/her as you did when you first met.

What did you do to light the romantic spark when you were first married? Revisit those moments by reminiscing or go to the actual place and relive it. Your relationship is like a garden; if it is unattended, it grows up in weeds. There's nothing pretty about an overgrown garden full of thistles and thorn bushes. In order to have a beautiful garden that flourishes, it needs water, sun, and tending. Cultivate the soil of your heart to prevent anything from taking root that shouldn't be there. Water your relationship with love and let the warmth of the Son cause it to bloom again. Allow the Lord to help you become a beautiful garden that people love to experience.

A lack of attention, time and nourishing of your relationship will break down communication with your spouse. When communication is broken, Satan tries to broaden the gap to make it seem impassable. When you are no longer standing as "one," you become vulnerable to all kinds of influences. That's why the Word says, *"Though one may be overpowered, two can defend themselves. A cord of three strands is not easily broken."* — ECCLESIASTES 4:12. It takes the strength of you, your spouse and God intertwined to withstand the battle that rages to destroy your marriage.

If you look back and realize the reasons you got married were selfish and immature, just give it to God. You can't go back and change anything from the past. But God can and will redeem your past if you give it to Him.

As an act of selflessness, ask the Lord to help you treat your spouse as a success. It's amazing how a person changes when they are selflessly loved and cared for. Goethe said, "If you treat a man as he should be, then he will become what he should be."

If you are in an abusive relationship, PLEASE seek professional help—even law enforcement if necessary—immediately.

Contact local support groups and safe houses where you can find protected shelter. If you have trustworthy friends, don't be ashamed to share your situation with them. Ask for prayer from your church. Work on your marriage within the safety of separation until all abusive issues are resolved.

Final Note: The secret ingredient to a successful marriage is to put God in the center. Build your relationship with Him. Picture a triangle. God is at the top point and you and your spouse are at the outer bottom points. The closer you are to the Lord at the top, the closer you will be to each other. Allow the Lord to keep your relationship joyful, alive and well.

Meditation Questions
Take time to examine your heart and fill in the answers

- **(Single)** What is true love to you? Explain.

  _____

  _____

  (Married) What is true love to you? Explain.

  _____

  _____

- **(Single)** Have you ever experienced true love with either God or other friendships? What were the elements of it? Is it still a vibrant relationship or has it faded?

  _____

  _____

  (Married) Have you ever experienced true love with either God, your spouse, or other friendships? What were the elements of it? Is it still a vibrant relationship or has it faded?

_____

_____

- **(Single)** What are the human elements of love you feel are missing in your life?

_____

_____

  (Married) What steps are you going to take to pursue and deepen true love with your spouse and the Lord? This may involve sacrifice, change of expectations, clearing the air of resentment, forgiveness, communication, serving them or expressing your true feelings.

_____

_____

- **(Single)** Are you developing depth in your significant relationships and with the Lord? This may involve sacrifice, change of expectations, clearing the air of resentment, forgiveness, communication, serving them or expressing your true feelings. What steps are you going to take to improve those friendships?

_____

_____

  (Married) Make a detailed list of all the things you love about your spouse and then make another list of the things that need improvement. Commit to pray for those things every day. Remember God is the only one who can change your spouse.

_____

_____

Prayer

As you read this prayer, make it your own.

(Single's Prayer)

> *Dear Lord Jesus,*
>
> *Your Word says that we "have not" because we "ask not," so I am deliberately asking. You know my great desire to find and have true love in my life. In our society, that desire typically means to be married. However, I realize marriage is not the only way to experience the fulfillment of giving and receiving true love.*
>
> *There is no greater love than to lay down one's life for one's friends. —JOHN 15:13[23]*
>
> *Show me how to be completely in love with You and know Your love for me. I realize if I don't know Your love, I am incapable of loving others and having intimate friendships. You are the only One Who can love me unconditionally. Even if others have rejected my love in the past, You have never rejected me. Your Word says in 1 John 4:18, "There is no fear in love. But perfect love drives out fear, because fear has to do with punishment. The one who fears has not been made perfect in love." Lord, would You perfect Your love in me so I am no longer afraid to experience true love... and so that I may generously receive it and freely give it away. (pause here and wait to receive His love)*
>
> *I know I am only completed in You and the total expressions of your Divine Nature rests within me. Because I am fearfully and wonderfully made by You, You already know the kind of person who would complement my uniqueness. I desire a friendship and/or marriage in which we enhance each other's strengths and strengthen each other's weaknesses.*

Nothing is hidden from You. You have seen my loneliness and understand my intense desire to have someone on this earth who is Your love, Your voice, and Your heart extended to me. Lord, would You bring that person into my life. Open our eyes so we can see each other. Your Word says in Psalm 68:6,[24] "God places the solitary in families and gives the desolate a home in which to dwell." I know You are faithful and I believe You want the best for me. Thank You, in advance for answering the cry of my heart.

In Jesus' Name, Amen.

(Prayer for a married person)

Dear Lord Jesus,

The Bible says that we "have not" because we "ask not", so today I am deliberately asking. My marriage isn't as vibrant as it should be. I need Your help. I realize I can't change my spouse, only You can do that. So, Lord, change me so I am used as a catalyst to usher in the love-filled marriage I so desire.

I want to be the Godly spouse You ordained me to be. However, in my weak moments I have fallen short of my potential. I desire to be one who speaks life and encouragement into my marriage relationship. Give me grace and strength to guard my words.

I know I am only "complete" in You. Nothing or no one can do that for me. I'm sorry for the times when I've tried to make my spouse (or anyone else) fill that void instead of You.

Show me how to be completely in love with You and know Your love for me. For if I don't know Your love, I am incapable of loving others and having intimate friendships. You are the only One Who can love me unconditionally. Even if others have rejected my love in the past,

You have never rejected me. Your Word says in 1 John 4:18 "There is no fear in love. But perfect love drives out fear, because fear has to do with punishment. The one who fears has not been made perfect in love." Lord, would You perfect Your love in me so I am no longer afraid to experience true love...and so that I may generously receive it and freely give it away. (pause here and wait to receive His love)

Nothing is hidden from You. You have seen my loneliness. I desire companionship and friendship in my marriage. I also need for You to show me how to enhance my spouse's life, calling and destiny. I want to be an encourager to him/her. Would You also give him/her the same desire toward me so that we can strengthen each other?

Lord, I need You to create a miracle of restoration to deepen our marriage relationship. I know You are faithful and I believe You want us to succeed. Thank you, in advance, for answering my heart's cry. In Jesus' Name, Amen.

Additional Scripture References

Take time to read these scriptures.

GENESIS 2:18—*The LORD God said, "It is not good for the man to be alone. I will make a helper suitable for him."*

PROVERBS 18:22— *He who finds a wife finds what is good and receives favor from the Lord.*

1 CORINTHIANS 13:13— *And now these three remain: faith, hope and love. But the greatest of these is love..*

JAMES 1:6— *But when he asks, he must believe and not doubt, because he who doubts is like a wave of the sea, blown and tossed by the wind.*

JOHN 16:24— *Until now you have not asked for anything in my name. Ask and you will receive, and your joy will be complete.*

JAMES 1:4— *Perseverance must finish its work so that you may be mature and complete, not lacking anything.*

1 JOHN 4:16-18— *And so we know and rely on the love God has for us. God is love. Whoever lives in love, lives in God, and God in him. In this way, love is made complete among us so that we will have confidence on the day of judgment, because in this world we are like him. There is no fear in love. But perfect love drives out fear, because fear has to do with punishment. The one who fears is not made perfect in love.*

Scripture to Memorize

1 CORINTHIANS 13:4-8— *Love is patient, love is kind. It does not envy, it does not boast, it is not proud. It is not rude, it is not self-seeking, it is not easily angered, it keeps no record of wrongs. Love does not delight in evil but rejoices with the truth. It always protects, always trusts, always hopes, always perseveres. Love never fails.*

Endnotes

[21]Scripture taken from the Amplified Bible, Copyright © 1954, 1958, 1962, 1964, 1965, 1987 by The Lockman Foundation. Used by permission

[22]Scriptures quoted from The Holy Bible, New Century Version, copyright © 1987, 1988, 1991 by Word Publishing, Nashville, Tennessee. Used by permission

[23]Scripture quotation taken from the Holy Bible, New Living Translation, copyright 1996, 2004. Used by permission of Tyndale House Publishers, Inc., Wheaton, Illinois 60189. All rights reserved.

[24]Scripture taken from the Amplified Bible, Copyright © 1954, 1958, 1962, 1964, 1965, 1987 by The Lockman Foundation. Used by permission

Chapter 6

SABBATH—WHAT'S THE BIG DEAL?

A SHORT TIME INTO OUR MARRIAGE, Carl and I began to struggle with *time*. Being from German and Dutch descent; we were anything but lazy. In fact, "driven" might be a better description of our personalities.

We tried to fix the problem by adding hours to our work day. We thought getting up earlier and staying up later might be the answer. It wasn't long before we realized that wasn't the solution either. It merely added to our fatigue.

Weeks and months rolled by without a single day off. We couldn't find time for each other, let alone time for the Lord. Long workdays zapped any motivation or energy for cooking, cleaning or laundry. Soon our house was a disaster. Everything seemed out of control as we raced to beat the clock.

As self-employed musicians, we accepted every work opportunity in order to pay the bills. But, all of those combined still didn't provide enough income.

I began working up to fifty hours a week as a sales representative, and still tried to juggle studio sessions. And we both volunteered nearly twenty-five hours a week on the church worship team. Carl had forty private drum students, and played in music clubs six or seven nights a week.

We had no time.

We were young and determined, like a train blowing full speed down the track, working hard just to make ends meet. We thought that was the only way to get ahead in life. At that point, we had no priorities established in our lives. We simply plowed ahead giving no thought to the collision course on which we were headed.

Before long, we began to crumble under the weight of a never-ending workload. Something wasn't right. It became increasingly difficult to keep our heads above the rising river of fatigue, discouragement and loneliness. We were not only missing each other but we were missing time with the Lord. The lack was affecting *everything* in our lives including our wedded bliss.

One night, exhausted and in tears, I laid in bed pondering what we could give up so we wouldn't have to continue working seven days a week. We felt trapped!

We had been reading the Word, searching for answers and—suddenly—there it was, right in front of our eyes:

...for six days work is done but the seventh day shall be your holy day, a Sabbath of rest to the Lord. —Exodus **35**:2

A revelation of Sabbath came tumbling out of heaven. Even God took a day off after He created the universe. And we had never tried it! No wonder our lives and schedules were such a mess.

The next day at work, the phone never stopped ringing. It was a hard day and nothing seemed to go right. Angry customers called with order complaints, the printing department had a breakdown and orders weren't shipping on time because so many people were out with the flu. Typically, I prided myself in defusing irritable customers, but that day, I felt like one of them. I wanted to pick up the phone and chew someone out for my problems too. But there was no one to call and no one to blame.

When the phone rang again, I answered and heard a familiar voice. Carl sweetly asked, " Hi honey, how are you doing today?" Drawn into the safety of his genuine concern, I couldn't hold back the flood of tears that had been locked behind a wall of professionalism. "I'm fine," I sobbed.

His calming tone rescued me once again as he said, "First of all, Honey, I am sorry things have been so hard lately. I know we've needed to make some changes in our lifestyle and I think I have an idea that will help. I feel like the Lord spoke to me and said I'm to give you permission to quit your job. And if you're OK with that, I think you should go ahead and give your two-week notice today."

"What?!"

After recovering from the shock, I had no doubt God had spoken and Carl had clearly heard from Him. For Carl Albrecht to say, "The Lord spoke to me…" was a miracle in itself; that wasn't language he typically used. Secondly, I knew he had to have heard from God because my German husband would *never* ask me to give up a cash-paying job! Never! Especially since I knew we couldn't make our monthly budget without my income. In fact, quitting my job had never crossed my mind as an option! In the natural, it was ludicrous so I knew it had to be a God-thing. I agreed to give my two-week notice.

Trying to constrain my mounting excitement, I slipped into my boss's office to tell him the news. Much to my surprise, he readily accepted my notice and said that if things didn't work out, I would be welcomed back. I wanted to scream! Not only was I relieved to be leaving the 8-to-5 grind but humbled at the realization that, even with my resignation, I still found favor with the company.

As I walked out of his office, I felt like a helium balloon that had just been untethered. Making my way to the car at the end of the day, I raised my eyes to the sky and I took a deep breath. The air smelled green with the life of spring and the sky was cloudless and blue.

Even though I had just quit my job, my heart was soaring with complete peace. I knew I had done the right thing and I felt the Lord's pleasure at our obedience. Responding to His directive and stepping out in blind faith was such an irrational thing to do. I decided not to tell anyone about our decision because I didn't want to hear rational caution. There was no logical reason for resigning, *especially* without a back up plan.

The events of the day had not taken God by surprise. He had been carefully watching over our lives, planning to rescue us from drowning in our over extended pursuit of success. He wanted us to acknowledge our need for His divine direction and assistance so He could help us stop the madness spiraling out of control.

The next Saturday morning our pastor's secretary called.

"I just finished a board meeting where you and Carl were one of the topics of discussion. We have been singing your praises for the great job you and Carl do on the worship team week after week; for being prompt and being available all the hours of rehearsals and services. We want to thank you for serving the church so graciously." Then she added, "Because we value what you do, we would like to know if you would be willing to receive a part-time salary for your time and effort?"

That in itself was shocking enough, but then she added the amount they wanted to pay us, it nearly took my breath away. Their part- time salary was going to be more than I had made at my full-time job! Clearly, the Lord was making a profound change in our belief system. He was reestablishing the fact that He cares about *every* detail of our lives.

As I hung up the phone, I didn't know whether to scream, laugh or cry. Overwhelmed by the goodness of God, I slumped into a chair next to Carl at the kitchen table and said, "You're not going to believe what I'm about to tell you." As I told him the news, we sat there, wide-eyed with our mouths hanging open. Too dazed to speak in complete sentences, we uttered short gasps and one-word exclamations like, "Wow!" and "Really?"

It was hard to believe that just the day before, we had taken a huge step of faith and in less than twenty-four hours God responded to it! What made it even more astounding is the fact that we had not shared our decision with anyone. No one knew about our desperate need. Only God!

Carl eventually reduced his student teaching load and Mondays became our cherished day off (a Sabbath does not have to be Sunday). Our relationship began to improve. Even when we had long days or short nights, the hope of a Monday Sabbath gave us the grace to keep going. At the beginning of a month, we wrote S-a-b-b-a-t-h across each Monday for it was our committed day of rest. That day became as important and guarded as any other commitment. Setting aside a Sabbath day carried us through to better days.

It wasn't long before the upheaval and disorder began to simmer down and our priorities began to take shape. The first thing I noticed was that I began to *like* Carl again. I always loved him but the time crunch and lack of attention to our marriage crowded out the "like" part.

Not only was I able to make our house a home again, but I also spent more quality time with the Lord. My relationship with Him began to take on a whole new meaning. His life poured into me. I found joy, rest, and deeper perspective on ordinary things. It seemed like my heart and body suddenly woke up from the dead.

Week Six   [Date: _____]

Pick one day out of your week when you can take time to sit and reflect on the following thoughts and respond to the meditation questions below.

Sixth Step to Becoming Free: *Consciously Begin to Rest in The Lord.*

Most of us twenty-first century, western civilization types multi-task. We juggle jobs, spouses, kids, school, friends, social activities, church, and ministries…and then there's the Internet, MySpace, Facebook, Twitter, websites, email and Google—just in case we have any left over minutes in our day. As we collapse into the bed at night, we sink into the pillow, hoping to drift into seamless sleep but our mind is still racing. We end up lying awake half the night, worried about how we're going to accomplish everything to which we've committed ourselves. When the alarm finally goes off in the morning, we're still exhausted and wonder if anyone got the license number of the Mac truck that seemingly ran over us in the middle of the night. As we stop to consider the insane pacing of our life, it's no longer a mystery as to why we find it increasingly difficult to do any one thing well.

What does a day of rest look like? The dictionary defines rest as: a period of inactivity, relief from anything distressing, annoying or tiring; to get refreshment by ceasing from work or exertion; to be at peace or tranquil or still for a while. I had no way to relate to that kind of day since I had never deliberately taken one with that perspective.

Taking a Sabbath wasn't as easy as we thought it would be. The habit of perpetual motion was hard to break. We constantly caught ourselves dabbling in business or attending to phone calls. And as soon as we decided to take a rest day, the enemy brought every kind of distraction in order to steal it from us.

However, as we discovered the benefits of taking a Sabbath, it became easier to put new habits into place.

I love the fact that the Lord rested on the seventh day. Why is Sabbath important? When we keep the Sabbath we enter into a blessing. ISAIAH 56:2— *Blessed is the man who does this, the man who holds it fast, who keeps the Sabbath without desecrating it.* The Lord promises incredible goodness to be released into our lives when we embrace the principle of resting.

God made the Sabbath for us. MARK 2:27-28— *The Sabbath was made for man, not man for Sabbath. So the Son of Man is Lord even of the Sabbath.* Jesus becomes our Sabbath rest. Whatever day of the week we commit to as a Sabbath, that becomes the Lord's Day for us. Of course, all our days are the Lord's but we determine to cease from labor on our rest day.

Taking a Sabbath day requires *trust*. Trust in God's ability to continue sustaining us and providing for our needs even when we are at rest. However, we have to decide to let Him do it. The only way to truly rest, body, mind and spirit, is to believe God will take care of us…even while we are resting.

Furthermore, working every day of the week holds no lasting benefit in the long run. Time and time again, Carl and I have proven the fact that our labors generate more income in six days than they ever do in seven days. When we take a Sabbath, it's as though our income is multiplied and He protects it.

Why is it important to trust? Trust requires faith and faith is the foundation to a passionate relationship with God. HEBREWS 11:6— *Without faith, it is impossible to please God.* As we learned through this experience, I believe our step of faith pleased God in our desire for a weekly Sabbath.

When I quit my job that day, we were walking in blind faith, totally dependent on God. He took what seemed to be a ludicrous decision and turned it into miraculous provision. It was evident our act of obedience in faith released a blessing into our lives. That miracle will forever be a benchmark in my life.

Nuggets of Truth

Helpful Guidelines for your Sabbath day of rest:

Carl and I shut down the computer and turn off the phones. We embrace restful things like lingering over a meal or a second cup of coffee, exploring our dreams and desires for the future, taking a nap or sauntering through the park. We open our eyes and ears and allow our senses to enjoy things we don't typically have time for. We deliberately devote our attention to each other and the Lord. Many times, we even take off our watches. On Sabbaths, our sole motto is: "Eat when you're hungry and sleep when you're tired." We give ourselves permission to do nothing but rest.

We tell our friends when we are taking a Sabbath so they know not to call us, unless of course, it's an emergency. We usually check our messages periodically but wait until the following day to resume business calls.

Obviously, if you are married or have children, a Sabbath day needs to be celebrated together. You can't just shut your kids in the closet and say, "Mommy and Daddy need a Sabbath so we'll see you tomorrow." Make every effort as a family to alleviate outside distractions…the things that continually pull on your attentions. Technology is a wonderful thing but never let it replace the organic art of conversation. Give yourself permission to have your own thoughts. Shut the television off and read together, go for walks, discover each other's dreams and desires by asking thoughtful questions. Then actually take the time to listen to what they have to say. Intentionally interact with each other. You will be amazed at how your love and relationships will deepen.

If you are single mother or one who is the sole caregiver for a sick spouse or family member, don't be afraid to ask others for help. Be creative. You may want to share the load with someone else who has a similar situation. Offer to help them out so they can also have a rest day in exchange for the favor. Many churches have "Mother's Day Out" which offers free childcare for a good portion of a day. Don't forget to pray and ask the Lord to bring people into your life that can help you.

It's important to put your life and priorities in order. The thing you give your most attention to is the thing that is a priority in your life. We have found when our priorities fall out of order, life begins to crumble which causes meltdowns. However, we find if we keep the following order in mind, life is less strained.

1) God—Maintain your relationship with Him daily

2) Spouse —Keep the channels of communication open, showered with lots of love

3) Children—More of the same from #2

4) Job—The occupation that pays the bills

5) Ministry—Your service to others. Of course, your whole life is a ministry but I am speaking of the volunteer time you give to your church, your friends and extended family or organizations that need your help.

If you are married, ask the Lord to move on your spouse's heart to pursue the same priorities. There have been times I knew I wasn't supposed to spearhead a change in our lives so I asked the Lord to speak to Carl about it, and He did. He can speak to your spouse, whether he/she is a Christian or not. Psalm 25:8— *Good and upright is the LORD; therefore he instructs sinners in His ways.*

Of course, if you don't have all these elements to consider because you are single or don't have children, simply skip those components. But whatever factors are in your life, give time and attention to them. Do it with all your heart.

We are also amazed at how much more we accomplish after a day off. Our minds and bodies are refreshed and we think clearer. Creativity has had time to incubate and begins to pour out in the days following rest. We continually marvel at the blessings that come from the obedience of taking a Sabbath.

He already provided for that day of rest and *commanded* us to take one. Take full advantage of it. Give your mind, body and spirit a chance to rejuvenate. He's got you covered. He's God and we're not so let Him do His job. Allow Him to be Lord over every part of your life...including your schedule, relationships, health and finances...and REST. He is a better time manager that we'll ever be. Give it a try.

Meditation Questions

Take time to examine your heart and fill in the answers.

- As you look at the things you give your attentions to, what are your priorities right now?

1) _____
   _____
   _____

2) _____
   _____
   _____

3) _____
   _____
   _____

4) _____
   _____
   _____

- How would you like your priorities to change and what changes are you willing to make for that to happen?

_____
_____
_____
_____

- Do you take a Sabbath every week? If not, what are some things you're going to let go of so you can start receiving the blessing of rest?

_____

_____

_____

_____

- Make a list of what you are expecting from the Lord by taking a Sabbath.

1) _____

2) _____

3) _____

4) _____

A Personal Note from Leann:

Maybe you are one who feels trapped in life. You can relate to the little furry animal that propels the hamster wheel. In fact, you can't remember the last time you took a full day off. You're aware the pace of your life is out of control but you don't know how to stop it. Something has to change.

If that's you, I believe God wants to intervene for you. Your life has been stolen from you and God wants to give it back. If you ask Him to intervene, He will. You don't need to continue life at a numbing pace. He is waiting to show Himself faithful by returning your joy, happiness, peace and a body that's alive again. Give God permission to make a way for you through this prayer.

Prayer

Dear Jesus,

I have tried to run my life my own way and it is careening out of control. I need Your divine intervention, right now. I have not been mindful to keep the Sabbath or to set my priorities straight. I want my life to change so I can have time with You and my family. Would You make it clear to me, which things I am to let go of and which things I am to hold on to. Only You can show me which responsibilities are important for me to keep. I want to surrender every part of my life to You including the management of my daily schedule. Lord, would you make a way so I begin to enter the blessing of keeping a weekly Sabbath; a time I can dedicate to You, my family and to rest. Help me to trust You.

I thank You in advance for the blessing and favor that will follow this decision of faith. I put You in charge of my life and thank You for turning it around for Your glory and the testimony of Your faithfulness. I give You all the glory for it.

In Jesus' Name, Amen.

Additional Scripture References

Take time to read these scriptures.

GENESIS 2:2-3— *By the seventh day God had finished the work he had been doing; so on the seventh day he rested from all his work. And God blessed the seventh day and made it holy, because on it he rested from all the work of creating that he had done.*

EXODUS 20:11— *For in six days the LORD made the heavens and the earth, the sea, and all that is in them, but he rested on the seventh day. Therefore the LORD blessed the Sabbath day and made it holy.*

EXODUS 31:13— *Say to the Israelites, "You must observe my Sabbaths. This will be a sign between me and you for the generations to come, so you may know that I am the LORD, who makes you holy."*

ISAIAH 58:13-14— *"If you keep your feet from breaking the Sabbath and from doing as you please on my holy day, if you*

*call the Sabbath a delight and the LORD's holy day honor-
able, and if you honor it by not going your own way and not
doing as you please or speaking idle words, then you will
find your joy in the LORD, and I will cause you to ride on the
heights of the land and to feast on the inheritance of your
father Jacob." The mouth of the LORD has spoken.*

EZEKIEL 20:20— *Keep my Sabbaths holy, that they may be a sign
between us. Then you will know that I am the LORD your God.*

MATTHEW 12:8— *For the Son of Man is Lord of the Sabbath.*

HEBREWS 4: 1-3— *For as long, then, as that promise of resting
in him pulls us on to God's goal for us, we need to be careful
that we're not disqualified. We received the same promises
as those people in the wilderness, but the promises didn't
do them a bit of good because they didn't receive the promises with faith. If we believe, though, we'll experience that
state of resting. But not if we don't have faith.*[25]

HEBREWS 4:4— *For in a certain place He has said this about the
seventh day: And God rested on the seventh day from all His
works.*[26]

Scripture to Memorize

HEBREWS 4:9-10— *There remains, then, a Sabbath-rest for the
people of God; for anyone who enters God's rest also rests
from his own work, just as God did from his.*

Endnotes

[25]Scripture from *The Message*, Eugene H. Peterson, 2002, Used by Permission
of NavPress, All Rights Reserved. www.navpress.com (1-800-366-7788)

[26]Scripture taken from the Amplified Bible, Copyright © 1954, 1958, 1962, 1964,
1965, 1987 by The Lockman Foundation. Used by permission

Chapter 7
COMING FULL CIRCLE

"WELCOME TO TAIPEI."

As we taxied to the terminal, the blood pulsating through my head was competing with the vibrating engines. Cold fingers of fear gripped me. Normally, after a long international flight, I couldn't wait to get off the plane. But that day was different.

When we parked at the gate, I knew the time had come. Within a few minutes I would have to face those who had devastated me not long ago.

I had no idea how I was going to face what lay ahead of me. Down the jet-way, along the corridors, collecting my luggage, and through customs I tried to remember scripture to give me courage. The only one that kept coming to my mind was ROMANS 8:28—*"All things work together for the good of those who put their trust in Him."* It didn't seem like anything good could come out of the mess I found myself in. I had no choice but to trust and wait to see what the Lord would do. It was hard to believe my experience was coming full circle and I was right where I started just months earlier.

I did everything I could to avoid going on the trip. I had begged Jake, the executive director, to dismiss me. He answered, "Leann, even though I know how painful it was for you, I think you should stay with the team." None of my fears and concerns seemed to dissuade him. His mind was made up.

Six months earlier I had left Taiwan devastated by the local church leaders. Through countless encounters, I felt bruised by the misogynistic prejudice and the disrespect of women in the Taiwanese culture. Even with Christians. In my leadership role with our team, I met continual resistance from the church pastors and leaders. At the end of the three-week tour, I felt like an abused wife.

In 1995, when Carl and I arrived on that first trip in Taipei, our music team had no idea what awaited us. Although we had traveled widely, that was our first time to visit Asia. We faced back-to-back conferences in several cities during the day and worship concerts nearly every evening. Our days started long before dawn and finished long after midnight.

The grueling pace of the tour and being the only female on the team were not what made the trip so hard. I had traveled often and extensively in ministry. In fact, I enjoyed adapting to different customs and cultures. I accepted it all as an exciting adventure. But the shocking conditions and traditions of Taipei kept me off balance and emotionally raw throughout the tour. I struggled to find peace in the midst of chaos.

Each day our commute was a kamikaze experience as vehicles defied the painted lanes on the streets. The sides of the van vibrated with the whir of mopeds, stacked with people, zipping by at breakneck speeds. I had never seen a family of five on one moped before! On many occasions, I closed my eyes, bracing for the screech of an inevitable crash. When I opened my eyes I saw hundreds of vehicles spilling chaotically through an intersection as our driver maneuvered effortlessly ahead.

Walking along the sidewalks, the sweltering heat intensified the stench of urine and sewer gas permeating the air of the city. We saw starving animals, covered with mange and sores, everywhere. As an animal lover, a sharp pain ran through my heart every time I saw a bony animal scavenging through trash. No one seemed to care about, or even see, them. Locals just stepped over them or angrily chased them away. I wanted to rescue each one of them, and did feed a few of them with my left over food.

In doorways of businesses and homes, we saw offerings of food and burning incense of remembrance for "Ancestral Worship." It was hard to believe that living people were idolizing urns of ashes from ancestors. The worshippers were as lost as those who had gone before them.

The skyline was etched with beautiful temples of carved wood and stone, shrines of worship to man-made gods. My heart saddened as I thought of the people trying to appease a god that was powerless to help them. As we walked into the evening, the heavy fragrance of incense wafted through streets like humidity after a summer rain.

In "Snake Alley" we saw pens of live snakes and furry animals being offered on the dinner menu. The sign on their cages read "Dressed and grilled while you wait." I had no sympathy for the snakes but I couldn't stand the thought of killing the beautiful pelted animals.

It seemed every captured animal species was a delicacy that had a superstition attached to it. For instance, some locals believed that eating the beating heart of a snake was an aphrodisiac. Their spiritual desolation hit me so hard as I gazed into the eyes of the empty souls wandering through the market. I was overcome with compassion for them. The Kingdom of Heavan was available to them, but they had no comprehension of it. I saw the culture desperately trying to find God in vain heathen rituals. Without Jesus, they were careening along a hopeless path, paved with tradition and superstition.

I saw the result of worshipping an idol made of stone. They had become like the thing they worshipped; they too had eyes that could not see and ears that could not hear. Since their spirits had never been awakened, they merely *existed* from the cradle to the grave. It was the first time I had witnessed a people group with such concentrated spiritual poverty. Less than one percent of the population were born again believers!

I didn't fare much better when I turned to the conferences. The volunteers worked so hard setting up PA systems and classrooms and providing meals and transportation for us. The dark circles under their eyes and long faces spoke volumes. So, I tried hard to not be a spoiled American guest. I made a valiant effort to eat the meals they served us. But, I often resorted to simply moving the food around with chopsticks, especially when they provided Styrofoam boxed lunches of rice and dozens of whole tiny fish with the heads still attached. After three weeks, all I wanted was a meal that wasn't staring back at me. I was no longer intrigued with shark-fin soup and had no desire to chew on another duck's foot or participate in the honor of "sucking of the fish head." Finally, we went to McDonalds one evening. But I lost my appetite when I looked up to see a mama cat and all her kittens through the clear ceiling panels above our table.

My adventurous spirit was gone.

Hoping to gain relief from the pagan culture, I turned to the local churches sponsoring the event. But, they seemed to host the same religious ghosts from my own childhood. I kept running into high walls of prejudice between men and women.

It seemed that women were to be seen and not heard. They were great worker bees but they were not allowed to have a voice. Women cowered and could not lead, speak, or express themselves openly—even in Christian conferences. Even guests, like me, were no different. Every time I addressed one of the men in leadership, he turned away from me. I thought maybe they had not heard me, so I spoke louder; still no response.

The sting of dishonor and prejudice slapped me hard. I screamed inside: "Am I invisible? Isn't it customary politeness to speak when you are spoken to?" But I held my tongue as daily offenses lifted me onto a tidal wave of despair.

When I pleaded my case to others, all I heard was, "That's just the way things are over here."

Finally, the last day of tour arrived. We had one more night of worship before we headed home. I couldn't wait to leave the place where all my senses wanted to recoil.

That evening, at the end of the concert, long speeches of adoration were lavished on each team member and generous gifts of appreciation were presented to each one. That was followed by bowing, smiles and audience applause. Everyone, including the promoters seemed pleased to have finished a successful conference tour.

Then, abruptly, the ceremony ended. I thought surely there had been a mistake. They had delivered the last gift to a male team member standing next to me. No one mentioned my name (and I had taught and sang among them for three weeks). They couldn't have missed me, I was standing right there on the platform with the rest of the team. How could they have presented gifts and applause to all the men and not even uttered a "thank you" to me?

Choking back the tears, I busied myself gathering up notes and music. Soon the effort to control my emotions gave way to a flood of tears. Shattered, I quietly disappeared into the darkness backstage.

Carl and the rest of the team were speechless. They had seen what had just happened but were helpless to do anything about it. The van was quiet as we returned to the hotel. My only comfort was visualizing our plane taking off the next day.

I was relieved when we landed in Los Angeles—back in the land of life, liberty, and the pursuit of happiness, regardless of gender or race. God bless America! Our whole team kissed the ground!

As soon as we arrived at our hotel, I told Carl I was going for a walk. It was a warm autumn day. Not knowing where I was headed, I stumbled upon an old road that apparently had been closed for a long time. Grass had grown up in the cracks and high weeds along the sides. I was glad to find a sanctuary from all the traffic and businesses nearby. I knew I had to conquer the seething monster inside me that was becoming more enraged with every mental replay.

I sobbed as I walked and vented my pain and anger: "Why did You send me to that nation to endure such humiliation and rejection? I do not understand this one. I don't see how anything good can come from this!" Wiping away the snot and sweat, I continued to pour out my frustration. "I know You love the Taiwanese people, but *I don't!* I don't ever want to set foot in that country ever again! Next time they need help, send someone else."

I was glad to be *alone* with my Lord. I didn't want anyone else to hear my rage or try to *fix* me. I needed the space to be me; I knew that He was not afraid of my honesty. I also knew He had a larger view. From His magnificent love for the world, He would help me.

Finally, the Lord responded and reassured me that the situation would eventually make sense. He gently spoke to my spirit, "I am the Potter and I am molding character into your life. You are on my potter's wheel right now. Allow my hands to smooth over the crumbled edges of your emotions, mend the cracks from the stress of this situation and wash you with My love and acceptance."

My heart grew calm as the Lord continued to speak to me, "Leann, I allowed you to experience the pain those women live with everyday. I wanted you to see and feel their world so you could begin to pray for their freedom. I want you to be a part of liberating them from their spiritual captivity and to pray for the release of their God-given destinies. I want women to be free to give voice to my Spirit for they exhibit a part of who I am. I created man *and* woman in My image. Without a display of both images in leadership, the church is lacking the full expression of Me."

Although I wasn't thrilled about the idea of *helping Him* with this assignment, by the end of the walk, a change started taking place. As the pain melted away by His touch, I drank in the sun; its warmth thawed my frozen soul. The weight that had been sitting on my chest gave way and I could once again take a deep breath. The world wasn't the angry place it seemed to be just an hour ago. I found a deep compassion and love welling up in my heart for the Taiwanese people. Strength and hope returned.

Still a little hesitant about my participation in His plan, I thought: *This is great. I can send my prayers to the other side of the earth! I believe in the power of prayer and as far as I am concerned, God can do the rest Himself.* I was convinced that was the best idea until four months later, when we received a phone call from our executive tour director who asked us to be a part of another trip to Taiwan.

In my mind, I could see Carl going on the tour, with me praying for the tour and for Taiwan—all from the safety and comfort of my home! But, Jake and the Lord pulled me from my comfort zone and persuaded me to go back to Taiwan. By the end of the conversation, I agreed to go with the team.

Landing in Taipei again. I still wasn't convinced I was ready for the trip as we piled into the shuttle van at the airport. I rode in silence. I felt like I was traveling back into the heart of darkness and dreaded what was in front of me. Within an hour, I would face those men who had slighted me and crushed my courage a few months before. Even though God had done a miraculous repair of my heart, I was afraid. I wanted to respond to them with a right attitude but I wasn't sure I could.

As the van pulled up to the front of the hotel, I saw a red carpet extending all the way to the curb. To me, it was the image of the blood of Jesus stretching out to greet me. Courage came.

Suddenly the door of the hotel swung wide and the three conference leaders walked toward us. My palms began to sweat. Frantically, I asked the Lord, "What do I do now?" He whispered, "Love them as I love them." I thought: *Well, if I were Jesus...and a guy, I would throw my arms around them and embrace them with warmth and affection.* That idea had to be from the Lord because it certainly wasn't anything I would have ever done in light of my past experience.

The day was chilly, so I had thrown a full-length tweed coat around my shoulders. As I stepped out of the van, the first gentleman came down the carpet to welcome me. In my enthusiasm to "be like Jesus" I threw my arms around him. Suddenly his slight stature disappeared under my heeled, five-foot, eleven-inch embrace. As we stood there, it must have looked like a very large person with four legs. At the exact moment we embraced, I felt something shatter as if a wall between us had just broken. The impact was so palpable it startled me! I had no idea whether he had felt the same surge of power but it didn't matter. I knew something had just happened in the supernatural realm. God had destroyed the wall between us and it came crashing down.

We laughed and my heart was instantly flooded with love and compassion for those men. Obedience had activated God's intervention that brought the fulfillment of my prayers. The supernatural transformation was completed as I walked down the red carpet, greeting each one of them as the Lord had prompted me—in and through His love.

Things were never the same after that moment. I was treated with the utmost respect and honor. At times, I was embarrassed by the favor I received. I knew God had redeemed my identity as a woman. They allowed me to minister with complete liberty.

During the tour, many women came up to me and said, "You move in such a boldness and authority. How do you do that? Would you please pray for me?" Already feeling the anointing and compassion for them, it brought me great pleasure to be a part of God's plan to release them into their God-given destinies.

God loves the Taiwanese people just as they are and so do I. Cultural differences and religious practices are typically an ethnic group seeking to find God in the best way they know how. This experience was my journey to wholeness and finding confidence in my identity as a woman in Christ. I was grateful the Lord showed me how to practically extend God's love to them within a culture that was alien to me.

He brought me full circle.

APPLICATION STUDY GUIDE

Week Seven   [Date: _____]

Pick one day out of your week when you can take time to sit and reflect on the following thoughts and respond to the meditation questions below.

Seventh Step to Becoming Free: *Allow the Lord to Produce Character and Hope in Your Life When Faced With Hardships.*

It's important to embrace the adversities of life. Whining, complaining and throwing temper tantrums do nothing more than make us wait longer to learn the lesson the Lord is trying to teach us. Trials and testing are *allowed* to touch us for a reason.

   God is a good God and as a good Father He wants us to grow up as mature believers. Sometimes it's easy to think that God doesn't love us because we encounter difficult challenges, but quite the opposite is true. Our spiritual muscle is a lot like our physical muscles. A muscle that has never encountered resistance remains flabby and has little strength or stamina. But when a deliberate strength training exercise is applied, that same muscle begins to take shape and has the ability to withstand force, pressure and stress. The same is true with our spiritual muscle. If we are never challenged and never meet with resistance, we would never have the chance to grow and become strong. Trials and tests help us to fully develop a deeper faith.

ROMANS 5:3-4— *Not only so, but we also rejoice in our sufferings, because we know that suffering produces perseverance; perseverance, character; and character, hope.*

JAMES 1:4— *Perseverance must finish its work so that you may be mature and complete, not lacking anything.*

   Warning: About the time you feel like you've learned a lesson well, the Lord will allow you to be tested on it again to solidify it.

Nuggets of Truth

My *initial* response to testing is not always joyful like it says in JAMES 1:2-4— *Dear brothers and sisters, when troubles come your way, consider it an opportunity for great joy. For you know that when your faith is tested, your endurance has a chance to grow. So let it grow, for when your endurance is fully developed, you will be perfect and complete, needing nothing.*[27]

I've found that if I relinquish my "rights" and humble myself, it's a lot easier for me to embrace doing things His way instead of my way. I had to let go of my control of the situation in Taiwan and realize I couldn't change a thing. By doing that, I allowed God to unfold *His* plan and I was changed by the hardship instead of being destroyed by it.

When we do things His way, we can't take credit for it because He accomplishes it through us. The final result is that He receives all the glory and our "take away" is maturity, wisdom and understanding. What we have learned becomes a benchmark in our faith and every time we give testimony of His faithfulness, others are empowered by it. If we allow Him to have His way, He will always bring a matter full circle. When the end meets the beginning, it reveals a greater dimension of His goodness, infallible character and love for us.

There is another unforgettable lesson I learned through this story. Not giving up was a key to victory….even though I wanted to quit a million times. I had a choice to make. Was I going to shrink back, give up and run when the monster of opposition raised it's ugly head, or was I going to humble myself and allow the Lord to battle for me? I chose to move in the opposite direction Satan wanted me to go. Even though I had not been honored on the first trip, I was determined to extend honor to those men on my return trip. The work God did in my heart was evidenced on the red carpet that day.

It always amazes me to see how God redeems seemingly horrible situations. Out of a broken place, God can establish a platform by which we are able to mentor and model a new position of freedom for others that would never have had depth without suffering.

Sometimes it's easy to look at people and accuse them of being the "enemy". However, don't be fooled, there is only one real enemy and his name is Satan. People may appear to be your enemy, but, in reality, it's Satan warring against you.

When we pray for a situation, make sure to separate the two. MATTHEW 5:43-45— *You have heard that it was said, 'Love your neighbor and hate your enemy. But I tell you: Love your enemies and pray for those who persecute you, that you may be sons of your Father in heaven.* Be deliberate to pray for and bless people...even if they are not treating you well. Ask the Holy Spirit how to pray for He knows exactly how to right the wrongs and bring restoration.

When God opens a door of ministry and establishes His authority over it, He makes no differentiation to gender, race, color or age. All He is looking for is a willing heart that says, "Yes, use me for Your glory. I'll go."

Paul puts it clearly in GALATIANS 3:27-29— *For all of you who were baptized into Christ have clothed yourselves with Christ. There is neither Jew nor Greek, slave nor free, male nor female, for you are all one in Christ Jesus. If you belong to Christ, then you are Abraham's seed, and heirs according to the promise.*

Meditation Question

Take time to answer the following questions and write down your answers.

1) What situation(s) of being persecuted, mistreated or dishonored have you faced or are you presently facing?

_____

_____

_____

_____

2) How have you responded to it? Do you feel that God is in control or are you trying to control it? Are you running from it, trying to bury your hurt OR embracing it with the realization that God will use it to shape your maturity?

_____

_____

_____

_____

3) What steps could you take to begin to allow God's plan and God's way in this situation?

_____

_____

_____

_____

4) Have you taken the time to ask God specifically for wisdom to know what action you need to take first? Have you searched the Scriptures for help? What answers have you found?

_____

_____

_____

_____

Prayer

As you read this prayer, make it your own. After reading the third paragraph take time to reflect on the progression of events that led up to this point in your life. When completing that process, move on to the rest of the prayer.

> *Lord, I am deeply troubled by the circumstance that faces me right now. Take me above the scrimmage line to see Your wonderful plan through this hardship because I know You have one. Restore Your peace to me so I can cease from the violent battle raging inside. I need You to save me from Satan who seeks to destroy my very existence. You are my only defender. I know You will fight for me in heaven and on earth. I choose to trust in Your unfailing love for me. My life and breath depends on You.*
>
> *Lord, I need Your help and ask for divine understanding and wisdom concerning (name the one who is persecuting you) _____. I do not have the answer to this situation but I know You do. I can only see things in part right now but You can see the big picture.*
>
> *If I have done anything that contributed to this difficult predicament, I ask You to reveal my wrongdoing. It is my desire to conduct all my relationships rightly before You. Thank You, Lord, for covering my mistakes with Your love and forgiveness.*
>
> *I humble myself and embrace the lesson You want me to learn through this circumstance. Give me Your heart toward (the persecutor) _____ and let me see (the persecutor)_____ through Your eyes. Speak clearly to me as I wait for Your direction and fill me with Your love that overlooks all offenses. I also need an abundance of grace to walk with right moral character.*
>
> *I release (the persecutor)_____ into Your hands. Do a mighty work of transformation in his/her life.*
>
> *Lord, I thank You for refining me through difficulties and building my testimony of Your faithfulness. I give You all the glory for the miracle of answered prayer. In Jesus' Name, Amen.*

Additional Scripture References

Take time to read these scriptures. They will strengthen and remind you of His promises to you.

HEBREWS 10:38— *But the righteous will live by faith and if he shrinks back, I will not be pleased with him*

HEBREWS 11:1— *Now faith is being sure of what we hope for and certain of what we do not see.*

EPHESIANS 4:11-14— *It was he who gave some to be apostles, some to be prophets, some to be evangelists, and some to be pastors and teachers, to prepare God's people for works of service, so that the body of Christ may be built up until we all reach unity in the faith and in the knowledge of the Son of God and become mature, attaining to the whole measure of the fullness of Christ. Then we will no longer be infants, tossed back and forth by the waves, and blown here and there by every wind of teaching and by the cunning and craftiness of men in their deceitful scheming.*

JAMES 1:4— *Perseverance must finish its work so that you may be mature and complete, not lacking anything.*

1 THESSALONIANS 2:4— *On the contrary, we speak as men approved by God to be entrusted with the gospel. We are not trying to please men but God, who tests our hearts.*

JAMES 1:12— *Blessed is the man who perseveres under trial, because when he has stood the test, he will receive the crown of life that God has promised to those who love him.*

Scripture to Memorize

ROMANS 5:3-4—*We also rejoice in our sufferings, because we know that suffering produces perseverance; perseverance, character; and character, hope.*

Endnotes

[27]Scripture from *The Message*, Eugene H. Peterson, 2002, Used by Permission of NavPress, All Rights Reserved. www.navpress.com (1-800-366-7788)

Chapter 8
THE QUEST FOR MOTHERHOOD

I FLOATED THROUGH OUR WEDDING DAY suspended in a bubble of joy. It had taken twenty-seven long years to finally walk down the aisle with my prince charming; it was hard to believe the day had finally arrived. He was so fine. I gently squeezed his arm to make sure he was real. He was the perfect match as we sang to each other and exchanged vows of promise.

Five years passed as our love grew and we settled into a sweet comfortable life with each other. Then one day a new longing began to tug at our hearts. We both agreed, even though our favorite pastime was to simply be together, it was time to bring another expression of our love into the world. Hope flickered at the thought of baby Albrechts running through the house some day soon.

But, after several years of trying to conceive, we found out I had endometriosis. Seeing the deep disappointment in our faces, my doctor quickly laid out a possible solution: "Let's do surgery and see what we find. If the disease and scarring are not too extensive, we may be able to reverse the damage and restore your ability to get pregnant." After a successful surgery, we headed home from the hospital with renewed hope. We faced six-months of hormone treatments. But, after that, he said I should be able to conceive.

Six months later, we were counting days and marking the calendar again. With each negative pregnancy test, our emotional roller coaster took another plunge into disappointment and tears. I was so frustrated; what was I doing wrong? It seemed unjust that so many people, who don't *want* children or *shouldn't* have them, were getting pregnant. Was God not taking notice of our desperation?

One day, the pregnancy test was pink—positive! Had our prayers finally been answered? A baby was finally on its way! But, wanting to let the joy of our miracle soak a little deeper, we decided not to share our good news with anyone. There would be time for others to celebrate with us but not just yet. We wanted to celebrate our love and "new life" as a couple; cuddling, laughing and dreaming of all the fun we would have with our new baby.

Several weeks later, I knew something was terribly wrong. By the end of the day, it was obvious my body could not hold on to our little miracle. I'm not sure what flowed heavier, blood or tears. In one day, the sweet glow of pregnancy had been replaced with a dark cloud of sadness. Carl tried desperately to comfort me, "I'm so sorry, honey. It will be all right, though; I'm sure there will be more babies to come. And you don't have to worry, I still love you. My love for you is forever. Whether we have children or not, *you* will always be *my* number one baby."

Several years later I got pregnant again. Still feeling the sting from the last pregnancy loss, I held my anticipation lightly. It wasn't long before my fragile hope was again swept away. My body released another unborn child. But, this time, I was in the middle of a dou-ble-header live worship event with Ron Kenoly and Don Moen. We were recording "Lift Him Up" and "Worship With Don Moen."

It was hard to even concentrate on singing. I almost passed out from the pain. I wanted to scream but, of course, couldn't. My conviction that the "show must go on" kept my feet glued to the platform. I remained at the microphone, tightly clinching my knees together to keep the traumatic expulsion from dripping on the floor. And at every break, I ran to the restroom to reinforce the layers of protection that miscarrying demanded. I don't know how I survived the hours of agony. Eight hours later, we finished the recording and rehearsals. I was exhausted!

As time passed, the longing for children persisted. We moved to Nashville and, in time, began to hear stories of successful pregnan-cies from a local infertility specialist. Bolstered with new hope, I went through another surgery. As the doctor gave us a wonderful report, our hope increased. Three years later, we still had not conceived so we began to look for other specialists.

A friend had become pregnant after undergoing treatment from another local doctor. So, we went to see him. But, after spending thousands of dollars and going through a myriad of tests, he came back with the final results. Lowering his glasses to peer over the rims, he said, "I'm sorry to tell you but you have waited too long. At forty-one years old, you're too old. At this point, there is nothing I can do for you. You would need to use an egg donor if we proceed with treatment."

An egg donor! The news hit me like a ball bat. I was outraged! *Too old! Too late! What do you mean? We have never stopped trying to get pregnant!* I wanted to say ugly things to him but I held my tongue. It wasn't his fault. He was merely reading the test results.

Months faded into years as we waited, trying every new science or alternative medicine that held promise. In spite of all our efforts, nothing and no one seemed to help. Well-meaning prophecies were spoken over us, "The Lord has heard your cry. Within the next *six months* you will be carrying a child. You will bear a boy child…. and then a girl." Still others prophesied, "I see a set of twins being born to you." I desperately wanted to believe those words but knew only time would reveal whether their words were from the Lord or just hopeful statements.

Some ministry trips took us to third world countries where we visited local orphanages. On two trips, high-ranking officials told us they could minimize expense and red tape if we found a child we wanted to adopt.

Even though Carl had a few reservations about adoption, he went with me to an orphanage. As we walked into the gated compound, we were shocked. Apparently, the attention needed for baby care was more than their small staff could handle. Tattered cribs lined the dingy concrete block walls. Blistering hot and humid wind blew through ragged sun-bleached curtains.

The terrible stench revealed that many babies were unattended and still lying in their own feces.

We heard stories about each baby. And each one was more heart wrenching than the next. Some infants were left on the steps of the orphanage or a local church. One mother had an affair while her husband was working overseas. Surprised by the news that he was coming home early, she had the premature baby boy ripped from her belly to avoid a beating and divorce. That baby was so tiny! He couldn't have weighed more than a few pounds. As I held his frail body, my heart broke. Tears rolled down my face and dropped on his pale skin. I wanted to save the helpless one...I wanted to rescue them all, but I was only one person and the need was great. Holding him close, I prayed, "Lord, have mercy on this fragile life. He is precious because You have made him, but he has very little chance of surviving. Please forgive those who threw him away. Even though these babies seem to have no more value than trash, they are Your handiwork and deserve a chance to live... and to know You." I held him in prayer a long time before lowering him back onto the soiled sheets.

As I picked up each baby, I asked the Lord, "Is this the one? Should Carl and I give our love to this child; to provide a home and a future for him?" To my surprise and disappointment, each time He gently said, "No." Even though He wasn't giving me the answer I wanted, I knew I was clearly hearing His voice. Every time I embraced His answer, peace filled my heart.

For ten years, the quest for children consumed our thoughts and prayers. When I was forty-three, the phone rang one day. One of my friends had been introduced to a girl who was pregnant and wanted to give up her child for adoption. I was cautiously optimistic because there was still one major issue concerning adoption that needed to be resolved. After our last visit to an orphanage, Carl admitted he was not sure he could bond with a child who was not his own flesh and blood. So, we talked it though and prayed. I wasn't worried about it because deep inside, I knew he would be fine. We had adopted two chocolate Labrador Retriever pups, and he was madly in love with them. How much more would his heart open to a child that responded to his affection and called him, "Daddy?"

While praying about pursuing the opportunity, the Lord spoke to Carl about his concern of bonding with an adopted child. He simply said, "I adopted you, didn't I?" That settled the issue for Carl. He was willing to proceed with the adoption. At that moment, we agreed to make the phone call to the pregnant mother. With each ring, my heart pounded faster until she answered the phone. I introduced myself and she said her name was April. I could tell she was trying to be brave but the tone of her timid voice portrayed a life of brokenness. She was only nineteen.

She explained her situation, "I already have a 20 month-old little girl who I love very much, but I can't support another baby. That's why I need to find a good home for my baby boy." Her continuing story broke my heart: "I've been pregnant before by my father, but this one is by my boyfriend. I've been living with him but things aren't going well. When he gets drunk, he is very violent and I'm afraid he is sexually abusing my little girl while I am at work." Trying not to show my horror, I forced myself to stay calm…at least on the outside. But, I was horrified to think of the hell and pain this girl lived with every day.

As we finished our conversation, my mind was heavy with questions. Even though I desperately wanted to help her, was it the Lord's *best* that we proceed with this adoption? Was it a trap? Did this mother just want a free ride? Were we ready to embrace the emotional risk and financial commitment? There were no guarantees, because she had the legal right to change her mind at any time and keep the baby.

We sought the advice of professionals and prayer from our intercessors. Our adoption counselors assured that, in most cases similar to this one, mothers generally go through with the adoption. After having one child, a mother realizes the overwhelming responsibility of caring for a baby. When another baby comes along, she is more willing to give it up for adoption. Those assurances gave us the courage to take the next step. We placed another call to April.

We told her we would like to pursue adopting her baby boy who was due in two months. When April agreed, we bought her two plane tickets to Nashville. She and her little girl were moving to our home. Within a few days, we met with an adoption lawyer. And as we prepared to get the legal documents in place, she served us with a huge stack of forms to sign. Our fingers cramped as we signed and signed and signed. The paperwork was more daunting than getting a home loan.

We also completed and passed the adoption agency interview that allowed us to start classes to help make the transition to parenthood. I wondered if we would ever complete the mountain of red tape. Even though it was overwhelming, we knew it would be worth it to have a baby Albrecht soon.

April, so pale, walked off the plane holding her daughter's hand. Although she was in her third trimester, she looked terribly thin. As we hugged each other, I could feel her body tremble. She was so frightened and her little girl hid behind her, clinging to her leg. As I looked at the two of them, I was moved with compassion. I wondered if anyone had ever loved and cared for this child… either one of them? She reflected the forsaken life she lived.

Arriving home, we tried to make her feel welcome and comfortable. While trying to be the gracious hostess on the outside, a wave of panic was building as the realization of responsibility suddenly hit me! Sitting in our living room was a toddler and a pregnant stranger carrying our new son. Until that point, little children and babies had never been a part of our world. I wasn't even sure how to entertain them. Why hadn't I made sure we had toys, crayons and coloring books? I was so glad she couldn't read my mind as I tried to get a grip on my emotions.

The next morning I fixed a delicious organic breakfast, thinking it would be a real treat for April to have home cooking. I learned pretty quickly that her food of choice was a bag of chips and a coke. She nibbled at the food and apologized for not liking much of it.

Later that morning, she showed us pictures of her most recent ultrasound. Looking down, she gently caressed her stomach and confidently said, "This is your new baby boy." I couldn't imagine giving away a child, but she appeared to be completely resolved to it. Carl and I had already agreed on a name. We told her his name would be Jonathan Zachary Albrecht.

The adoption counselors suggested that instead of living with us, we should help her relocate to a home for unwed mothers. They warned that living in the close confines of our home might open the door for unwanted attachments. April could begin to look at me as her mother instead of me being the mother of her child. We took their advice and got her settled into a nice home on the other side of town. Since April didn't have a car, I took her to her doctors' appointments. We spent countless hours getting acquainted in waiting rooms and birthing clinics. It was a whole new experience for me. I had no idea a baby could be delivered with the mother sitting, standing, squatting or submerged in a bathtub! Amazing! I was leaving it up to April as to which method was most comfortable for her and how much she wanted our involvement in the delivery.

As the baby grew, so did our excitement. Friends were anxious to throw baby showers. With each kind invitation, I was hesitant and found myself saying, "No, let's wait. I just don't feel we are to receive gifts for Jonathan yet." I couldn't explain it. I don't know what I was waiting for but I knew the Lord would give me peace when it was time to prepare the house for the baby. In department stores, I circled racks of adorable baby clothes and the Lord would stop me. It was so odd; He wouldn't even allow me to buy one pair of booties! However, I trusted He had a plan and even though I had no clue what He was doing, I decided to obey and wait.

On a cold November morning, four weeks before April's Christmas due date, I picked up April and headed for the doctor's office. I was so excited that day because the doctor was going to do an ultrasound. I was going to get to see our little Jonathan for the very first time. As I stood at April's side, the bright screen of swirling images transmitted a moving form. The technician pointed out his head and hands and commented that everything looked great. Moving the wand from side to side, she suddenly stopped and exclaimed, "Oh yes...there you can see...it's a boy alright!" Finishing the exam she added, "Everything looks completely normal, April. I'll see you in a few weeks."

All of a sudden I felt uneasy. Instead of being elated by this incredible moment, my heart was heavy. As the doctor wrapped up the final instructions for April, the Lord spoke to me, "April has changed her mind." I didn't want to believe it and desperately hoped I had misunderstood Him, but it became glaringly apparent I had heard clearly. The ride home was silent.

The next morning a call from the adoption lawyer confirmed my greatest fear. She said, "April can't go through with the adoption. She has decided to keep the baby and asked that I call and tell you." As I hung up the phone, I stood there frozen. It seemed the chilling news had turned my blood to ice. Through the deep pain of disappointment, I groaned a mournful call to Carl who was downstairs. He came running and I told him the news.

Even though I heard the Lord tell me that April had changed her mind, I wasn't willing to accept it. *I wanted the baby.* "Surely, the lawyer has misunderstood," I blurted out. Then trying to find words to right the wrong, I cried, "Let me call April and try to reason with her. Maybe I can convince her to change her mind."

I could tell when she answered the phone she dreaded my call. I pleaded with her to reconsider, "Are you *sure* you want to do this?" Her mind was made up. In the last month, her love for the baby had grown and seeing him again made it impossible to give him away. With much regret, she concluded our conversation, "I have to keep my baby. I'm so sorry."

It was obvious nothing I was going to say would persuade her otherwise. Reeling from the blow of reality, I fell into Carl's arms and cried out loud. I suspected something because the Lord had warned us to wait on baby showers and gifts. But, still, we weren't prepared for the sting of April's final decision.

Through the sobs, I blurted out, "God, why did you give us your peace to proceed with this adoption? Why did you allow us to go this far? Our baby was so close! Our hearts were opened and we fell in love with this unborn child." I was sad, I was heart-broken, I was mad; I wanted answers! It felt like God had simply played with our emotions. As I poured out my tears and the wave of anguish crested, deep down inside His reassurance began to resonate. I knew He understood my broken heart and somehow He had a bigger purpose than I could see. In that moment, my hindsight of the Lord's faithfulness held me as an anchor of hope.

That Christmas didn't hold the magic of years past. We had no desire to decorate the house, hang lights or put up a tree. It was supposed to be the year we received the most precious gift of all…. a gift of a new life in our home. But that dream had slipped away again. Even the consoling words of friends and family couldn't erase the sadness.

April and her babies were last seen by some of our friends at a small local church. After that, they disappeared from Nashville without a trace. I often found myself fretting with unanswerable questions. "Where did they go? She couldn't take care of her first child. How was she going to take care of the second one?" Carl and I could have given Jonathan a rich life of love and affection. Maybe someday it would all make sense.

One year later, on a chilly January day the phone rang. The voice at the other end said, "Leann, this is April." After an awk-ward silence, she continued, "There's not been a day that's gone by that I haven't thought about you and Carl, and how sorry I am that I hurt you." Pausing for a moment she then continued by saying, "In fact, I pray for you everyday that God will give you children of your own." As I listened, my heart softened with her sincere concern and apology.

She told me where she was living, and how her life had changed since we had met. Then she said, "I also want you to know that I would never have known Jesus if I had not come to Nashville. I am forever grateful that you and Carl pointed me to Him." Like reopening a locked book of memories, I suddenly recalled the hours of intense ministry and prayer with her in our home. Then, she proudly added, "Because of you, I am raising both of my children in church. We go every week. In fact, my little girl is getting baptized this Sunday and as soon as my boy is old enough, he will be baptized too."

As I listened to her incredible story of spiritual awakening, my deep pain began to heal. Suddenly, I could see it from God's view. It even made sense. The experience was *so* much more than us adopting a son. It was the beginning of a redeemed legacy for an entire family! That was big! Finally, I saw God's plan and I understood the purpose for our suffering. The mystery was over.

After that ordeal, we never had the desire to pursue another adoption. We have two of our own miscarried babies in heaven being raised by the ultimate parent, Jesus. My heart beats with great anticipation when I think of meeting them some day.

And, I smile when I think of gazing into their sweet faces. They'll look a little bit like Carl and a little bit like me.

Week Eight   [Date: _____]

Pick one day out of your week when you can take time to sit and reflect on the following thoughts and respond to the meditation questions below.

Eighth Step In Becoming Free: *Let Go of The Things You Can't Control.*

In life, there are prayers and petitions that *seem* to go unanswered. I have learned that God's ways are not my ways and His thoughts are much greater than mine. Since He has the vantage point of life, I have to trust that He will unfold every detail of His plans for me as He sees fit. I can also trust it will be better than what I could have imagined. These two scriptures remind me of His Sovereignty. PROVERBS 16:9— *In his heart, a man plans his course, but the LORD determines his steps.* And PROVERBS 19:21— *Many are the plans in a man's heart, but it is the LORD's purpose that prevails.*

I can ask the Lord for answers but if He chooses not to respond right away, I must be content to wait and trust. If I want to remain in perfect peace, I have to let go of the things I can't control.

I may not know His reasoning on a matter this side of heaven, but I know one day, as I sit at His feet, He will explain all the mysteries of life. I know everything will make perfect sense when He reveals His divine purposes and plans for my journey on earth. I can trust His love for me and He will not disappoint my hope in Him.

Nuggets of Truth

I draw great strength and comfort from ISAIAH 54:1— *"Sing, O barren woman, you who never bore a child; burst into song, shout for joy, you who were never in labor; because more are the children of the desolate woman than of her who has a husband."*

Even though I didn't raise a child from birth, I still remain content and complete as a woman. Bearing children does not define my womanhood. Being a "mother" is one who nurtures; who has the responsibility and authority of a mother. A "mother" can also be defined as a "woman of influence". Every woman has the opportunity to be a "spiritual mother" and you can be one at anytime for the rest of your life. There are no age limits and no time clocks ticking!

Whether we have natural children or spiritual children, it's important to remember they are gifts from the Lord and are loaned to us here on earth. I believe our responsibility is to nurture them in a way that instills character for His glory. It requires us to draw on the strength and wisdom of God to know how to build their lives upon Godly foundations based on the Word.

No matter what age we are, I believe one of the main purposes in life is to mentor, impart the warmth of friendship and kindness to lonely hurting hearts. I keep in mind our lives on earth are but a blink in the span of time. While we are here, we must spread our arms wide open to change someone else's world with our love and encouragement. They need us…and we need them.

Meditation Questions

Take time to explore your heart and true feelings. Then write them down.

1) What does being a parent mean to you?

_____

_____

_____

_____

2) Whether you have natural born children or spiritual children, how can you better influence their lives in a positive way?

_____

_____

_____

_____

3) Now that you realize the definition of a "mother" is
   not limited to a woman who bears a child, what acts
   of kindness and love can you begin to show to those
   around you? Take time to allow the Lord to give you
   some new ideas.

_____

_____

_____

_____

Prayer

As you read this prayer, make it your own. Fill in the blanks with
your children's names. If you do not have natural children, fill in the
blanks with the names of those who are influenced by your love
and care.

> *Father, In Jesus' Name, I draw on Your strength and con-*
> *fess Your Word over my leadership as a parent or guardian*
> *over my child. _____ is a precious gift to me and I*
> *am grateful You have entrusted him/her to me. I am com-*
> *mitted to train _____ in the fear of the Lord. Help me*
> *to be faithful and consistent with my discipline and love*
> *toward him/her. I want to be careful not to provoke or*
> *discourage him/her in any way. My desire is to encour-*
> *age and admonish him/her to maturity. When I am over-*
> *whelmed or discouraged with motherhood, counsel me*
> *and give me strength to see _____ through Your eyes.*
> *Pour out Your unconditional love through me. I know You*
> *will perfect all things that concern me. I commit the cares*
> *of raising _____ to You. He/she is in Your hands and I*
> *trust Your ability to carefully watch over and guard him/*
> *her. Station angels around him/her to keep him/her safe*

from the attacks of Satan.

I am fully confident that all the days of _____ life are ordained by You. His/her God-given destiny is secure in You. Give him/her a heart that is steadfast so that he/she will live a life of true joy and fruitfulness. Thank You, Father, that You have heard my prayer. I can rest knowing You will carefully attend to all of these details. In Jesus' name, Amen.

Prayer for women who desire children:

Jesus, I thank You for the relationships and family that currently exists in my life. At times, however, I am sad because I don't have children. I know that children do not "complete" me as a woman and mother because the full expression of Your Divine Nature rests within me just as I am. However, as one who is an extension of You, I have a deep longing to love, care for and provide for children who need love.

At this point, I have not been able to see that dream fulfilled. I need Your help. Lord, would You do a creative miracle between my husband and me so we are able to conceive, open the opportunity to adopt a child, or send us spiritual children who need nurturing.

I know Your plans for me are perfect and I trust You will "settle" my longing for children. I relinquish this desire to You for I know it will be satisfied in Your flawless timing and in Your perfect way.

Thank you for answering my prayer. In Jesus' Name, Amen.

Additional Scripture References

Take time to read these scriptures. They will strengthen you as you are reminded of His promises to you.

PSALM 113:9— *He makes the barren woman to be a home-maker and a joyful mother of spiritual children. Praise the Lord! Hallelujah!*

ISAIAH 66:13— *As a mother comforts her child, so will I comfort you.*

PSALM 128:3-4— *Your wife will be like a fruitful grapevine, flourishing within your home. Your children will be like vigorous young olive trees as they sit around your table. That is the Lord's blessing for those who fear him.*

PSALM 127:3— *Behold, children are a heritage from the Lord, the fruit of the womb a reward.* [28]

ISAIAH 55:8-10— *"For my thoughts are not your thoughts, neither are your ways my ways," declares the LORD. "As the heavens are higher than the earth, so are my ways higher than your ways and my thoughts than your thoughts."*

COLOSSIANS 3:21— *Parents, do not be so hard on your children that they will give up trying to do what is right.*[29]

EPHESIANS 6:4— *Fathers, do not irritate and provoke your children to anger and do not exasperate them to resentment, but rear them tenderly in the training and discipline and the counsel and admonition of the Lord.*[30]

Scripture to Memorize

ISAIAH 54:1— *Sing, O barren one, you who did not bear; break forth into singing and cry aloud, you who did not travail with child! For the spiritual children of the desolate one will be more than the children of the married wife, says the Lord.*

Endnotes

[28]Scripture taken from the Amplified Bible, Copyright © 1954, 1958, 1962, 1964, 1965, 1987 by The Lockman Foundation. Used by permission

[29]Scripture from Contemporary English Version (CEV), © 1991, 1995 by American Bible Society. Used by permission. All rights reserved.

[30]Scripture taken from the Amplified Bible, Copyright © 1954, 1958, 1962, 1964, 1965, 1987 by The Lockman Foundation. Used by permission

Chapter 9
No Place Like Home

WHEN I WAS YOUNG, HOME WAS A REFUGE TO ME. That haven of rest was always complete when mom greeted us with a warm hug and a heartfelt question, "How was school today?" Every day, that ritual celebrated our return home. On laundry days, she was outside hanging clothes on the clothesline. The smell of fresh laundry was invigorating as I raced through the tunnel of sheets, trying not to get tangled up between unpredictable gusts of wind. But, on other days she already had dinner started. It wasn't long before the aroma of fried chicken, a fresh catch of the day by the local fishermen, or a pie in the oven would waft through our house.

On special occassions, Mom made my favorite dessert, cream puffs. We weren't allowed to have one before dinner, but if I hung around while she made them, she let me lick the custard from the spatula. At the end of the meal, as mom brought the platter of fresh cream puffs to the table, I sat up straighter and leaned in to view the spendor. My sensory world was satisfied as I took the first bite of a crisp egg pastry brimming with warm vanilla pudding. Closing my eyes, I savored the buttery sweetness that squished between my teeth. As soon as I devoured the cream puff, I reached for another one.

When we finished, we helped mom clear the table. Then it was time for homework. Dad often went to the tool shed to tinker with something that needed fixing or to his study to prepare a Sunday sermon. As soon as I finished homework, I went to look for him. I loved finding dad. Our eyes met when he looked up to greet me and I felt his love, resting in the gaze of his smiling blue eyes. Then he would say, "How's my girl today?" He often tried to show me what he was working on. I really didn't want to know how to fix a lawn mower engine or change the oil in the car or outline a sermon. I just wanted to be close to him for a little while before I went to bed.

It was easy to feel the emotional connect of home while I lived with mom, dad and my brother. We were always there for each other and home was where my heart found love. Something about *home*—our home—captured the warmth and security that reflects our heavenly home. I think we all reach for that throughout our lives. And, a desperate longing emerges when we don't find it. The search for that place was always with me as I became an adult.

When I moved out on my own, it became more difficult to find that familiar place with a sense of security. My career choices didn't help much. Traveling jobs made it difficult to cultivate a consistant circle of friends. I longed for that emotional sanctuary but tried not to stress over it. I knew someday I would again find that "center" called home.

For the first years of my young adult life, I led a gypsy lifestyle. Then my world changed with Carl Albrecht. He was the first guy who ever made me want to settle down and start a family of our own. On June 16th, 1984, we made it official.

Returning to St Louis from our honeymoon, the "nesting instinct" kicked in. Decorating our small rental home was a spontaneous adventure as we discovered each other's individual tastes. We quickly found I liked to decorate in sets of odd numbers and angles while he liked things in even numbers that were perpendicular.

One of our biggest fights was about the bathroom. I liked the bathroom towels straight. His were chaotically thrown over the towel bar. We eventually compromised our differences and soon our tidy love nest was decorated in early American garage sale with a thrift store motif. Finding a couch on a limited budget was a challenge until we found just the right one at Goodwill. We laughed all the way home with it strapped to the roof of my Honda Civic.

Three years later, in 1987, we bought our first home. It felt like I was finally settling into that long-awaited secure place. However, after living in our little house for five years, Carl and I felt the Lord prepare our hearts for a move when all of sudden, St. Louis didn't feel like home anymore. We couldn't explain what had happened but something had changed. Carl and I were still in love with each other, but when we came home it didn't feel the same. It felt like our house belonged to someone else.

We felt He was moving us for greater music opportunities in either Los Angeles, New York, or Nashville. I had lived in New York and knew we didn't want to live there again. A producer in California invited us to move there. So, we flew out for a visit. While staying with him for a few days, the Lord made it clear that Los Angeles was not our home either.

For a while, we had traveled to Nashville for recording session work. One evening as I was flying back to St. Louis, I looked out and saw the Nashville lights fading in the distance. When tears started running down my face, I wondered what was wrong with me. Then the Lord said, "Nashville is your home." I couldn't wait to tell Carl. When I got home, to my surprise, the Lord had already spoken the same thing to him.

With a van and trailer packed to the ceiling, we finally arrived at our new Franklin address, twenty minutes south of Nashville. Our small but adequate apartment sat high on a hill. I was so thrilled because it had a balcony that looked westward. We loved to sit out there and watch the sun set into the evening haze. It seemed to change into a puddle of red right before it said goodbye. As wonderful as the view was, I longed for my own yard, and walls that didn't rumble with boom cars driving through the parking lot at night. All I wanted was a place to call our own to start a family.

Less than a year later, we rented a three-bedroom house on a corner lot with lots of green grass, complete with huge shade trees and flowering bushes. It was such a relief to finally have more space where we no longer had to maneuver around stacks of Carl's drums and equipment. Our landlord, an elderly gentleman, was very gracious and gave me permission to plant a few flowers and vegetables.

But, before long, the airport opened a new runway and our house was in the direct path of air traffic. If we were outside, it got so loud that we had to stop any conversation until the plane had passed. And, inside the house, the windows vibrated and the walls rumbled. Our nerves started unraveling as the noise pollution took it's toll. It was time to find a quieter place to live.

Each Sunday, after the pastor's final "amen" and a quick lunch, we raced home and crawled up into the couch cushions with the Sunday paper. When I spotted an interesting property, I read all it's charming qualities aloud with theatrics, hoping to spark Carl's interest. Each time, however, he completely deflated my excitement by saying, "Honey, you know, there is no way we can afford to buy a house right now. Our free-lance income is so unpredictable." Even though I knew he was right, I didn't stop believing… or looking. I drew on God's track record of faithfulness. I knew our financial situation would change someday and we *would* find the house of our dreams…a place to call home.

Our opposite personalities seemed to balance our marriage. Carl always wanted to play it safe, and I was always daring to believe and live on the edge of possibility. I often became frustrated with his seeming lack of faith and willingness to step out of his comfort zone to ask the Lord for certain things….especially finances. I knew God cared about the desires of our heart, and I often felt He was merely waiting for us to ask.

One day, I decided to give up the pursuit. I simply prayed, "Lord if you want us to have a home of our own, then you can change our financial situation and Carl's heart to be open to looking for one. I'm going to lay it down. I want his agreement so we can discover this hidden treasure together." I immediately felt His pleasure as I relinquished my desire to Him.

Two weeks later, Carl and I were to leave for an Integrity concert tour in Scotland. So, we decided to leave a few days early to take a much needed vacation before the tour started. After we landed in Glasgow, we rented a car and drove for hours through narrow winding mountain roads, finally arriving at our lodge.

It was the hunting lodge of King Henry the VIII, nestled in the Highland Way. Travel book photos of a rustic palatial estate seemed the perfect place to get away. My imagination raced ahead to hallways adorned with portraits of royalty who had made history there. I couldn't wait to walk the corridors that once echoed the clumping of hunting boots worn by kings and noblemen. And sit near the fireplace that warmed them while they had a pint of ale to celebrate their trophy game.

Arriving in the faded light of evening, I suddenly realized my imagination was much different than reality. The "ancient and old" description was definately accurate! The weeds in the walkway and paint peeling from the front door reflected the years lacking the king's wealth.

A couple of days into our vacation, Carl woke up one morning very sick. We were many miles from any town or doctor. Instead of panicking, we decided to spend the day resting and waiting for his healing to come. The hours crept by as I nursed his flu symptoms with lots prayer, water and a bowl of bland cabbage soup from the kitchen downstairs.

As daylight faded, I rummaged through my luggage in search of a teaching tape, from our church, that I had thrown in at the last minute. I popped it into the player we brought. As our pastor talked about the faithfulness of the Lord, the Spirit began to speak to me about my desire to have a place called home. All of a sudden I was no longer listening to the tape but had tuned into the Lord. He spoke intently to me and said, "Finding the place you want will take a miracle. Keeping it will take another miracle of supernatural provision....but don't worry, I will provide all of it for you."

When Carl woke up the next morning, he was completely well! We were ecstatic the Lord had heard our prayers. He had once again been faithful to us! While we got ready for the day, I was aware of the seed of faith the Lord had planted in my heart the evening before. Throughout the day, the Lord reminded me of it and each time He did, my hope grew and I became more expectant. As we walked along the mountain top, on the Highland Way, the Lord told me not to bring it up again with Carl. It was as though the Lord was saying, "Let Me unfold My word, in My way and in My timing. You don't need to say another word to anyone about what I spoke to you. Let Me surprise you with how I will fulfill My promise." It felt like I was being carried on the wings of assurance like the clouds being carried on the wind that passed below us. I knew God was about to perform another miracle in our lives.

After completing the concert tour, we returned home on Sunday. Before we went to sleep that night, Carl said, "Why don't we get up in the morning and look for a house?" I was so shocked by what he said, I nearly fell out of bed! "Really?" I couldn't believe my ears. Before that moment, he had never mentioned any interest in looking for a home. I smiled in the darkness and whispered to the Lord, "You're truly amazing! Only You could have opened Carl's heart." It was barely two weeks since the Lord had spoken to me. He was working fast!

At the first light in the morning sky, I was out of bed! Not even exhaustion and jet lag could keep me down. Carl never ran full steam until noon, so I knew I had to do something special to get him going. Soon the aroma of bacon in the skillet and strong coffee pulled him from the pillow. The first miracle was taking place right before my eyes. Carl was out of bed, dressed and ready by 8:00 AM!

When we arrived at the real estate office, we entered our entire "wish list" data into the computer. There was one final detail to enter before the computer could calculate the information: price. Looking at each other, we paused. Then I heard the Lord say, "Take off the cap," which meant put in a higher number than we had initially agreed to spend. Stepping out in faith, we dared to do what the Lord said. The computer printed a list of twenty properties with specifications that would fit what we were looking for.

The day turned stormy; wind and rain pelted the windshield, making it hard to see. Many of the listings had pictures that looked appealing. However, as we drove to the front of each property, we would simultaneously and emphatically say, "Nope, this is definitely *not* the one!" We laughed out loud as one house was right next to a rooster farm while several others faced the interstate. We were looking for a haven of peace not a land of commotion!

Late in the day, after driving many miles on winding roads, we were tired and discouraged. It seemed like what we were looking for didn't exist. We had covered Nashville without so much as one prospect. As sheets of rain were once again pounding our windshield, we pulled into a parking lot to take a break. Annoyed and exhausted, I quietly muttered, "There's only one more house on the list and it's right down the street from here."

We drove down a long lane to the last house. As we came into the clearing, we stopped the car and sat in disbelief. There it was! We saw the house we had been looking for. Glancing back at the listing in my hand, I said, "Oh my gosh…this price can't be right! Maybe it's a misprint…if it's the right price, there must be something wrong with the house. Maybe the inside is a disaster because the outside is impeccable!" Then we looked again. Thinking we had the wrong house, we drove back down the lane to double check the address at the entrance.

The yard was beautiful and elegantly manicured. Although the property was only five minutes from the major conveniences of city life, it was so tucked away in the woods, it felt secluded and rural.

We both laid awake that night, imagining what it would be like to live there. Eventually we drifted into a happy slumber, knowing the morning would be bright with the possiblity of a new home.

The agent and the owner met us at the front door the next morning. As we entered, I could see it was not an ordinary house. The rambling floor plan certainly didn't reflect the typical farmhouse style. It had it's own unique country charm and it was in immaculate condition. Standing in the middle of the yard, Carl and I felt such peace; we sensed a "yes" from the Holy Spirit. He was giving His OK for us to buy it.

With our friends and agent, we headed to a nearby restaurant where Carl and I started the paperwork for an offer on the house. Rather than trying to negotiate a lower price, we both felt like we should agree to the asking price. So, we signed the papers. The next day, the agent called, "Congratulations! Although there were three previous contracts on the house, your offer has been accepted!"

With the help of friends, we moved in on Halloween. Even though the air was thick and cold, nothing could dampen our spirits as we unloaded in the rain. That evening, after the last box was carried in and our friends left, we stood in silence trying to absorb the goodness of God. A pair of night owls echoed through the foggy valley. Crickets and tree frogs struck the beginning chords of a nighttime symphony that beckoned our slumber. We would unpack at dawn's light, but that night, we rested in a chamber of answered prayer.

The next morning, the sun was bright and the sky was crystal blue. In the crisp fall air, Carl and I grabbed a bottle of oil and walked the perimeter of the property. As we walked, we prayed and anointed the corner fence posts with oil, stationing angels around our property and dedicating it to the Lord.

A few months later, a friend who is a prophet and seer came to visit. He said that he saw many angels on our property. As we talked, I asked, "Why do you suppose there are so many angels here?" He replied, "Well it's obvious, they and the Lord are welcome here. I suspect it is a resting area for angels because it is a safe place." That reality was thrilling to me. When we bought our home, I knew we would be hosting people from all over the world but it never crossed my mind we might also host guests from another world.. What an honor! In the fifteen years of living here, we have encountered our angelic guests on numerous occasions.

Wherever we are, Carl and I always look forward to coming home. Especially in the spring when everything is in bloom. My heart beats a little faster when I turn into our lane. I roll down the window to take a deep breath, allowing all my senses to register the healing silence that surrounds me and to savor the sweet smell of honeysuckle. The cool fresh air blows through my hair, sweeping away the weariness of travel; I am home!

As I walk through the door, the familiar—childhood and eternal—feelings of safety and peace capture my heart. Even though I am not a little girl anymore, I still welcome the same sights, sounds, touches and aromas that comforted me as a child. I'm sure they will also surround me in Heaven. But, for now, 405 Forrest Drive is our resting place. A spot on earth where Jesus is our rest, our peace, our True Home.

Week Nine [Date: _____]

Pick one day out of your week when you can take time to sit and reflect on the following thoughts and respond to the meditation questions below.

Content Point:

Ninth Key To Becoming Free: *Believe That God Wants to Bless You.*

Through the years, I have heard many teachings and read scripture about God's concern for the details of our lives. I often found myself chasing after *things* to make me happy. But, after reading this scripture, the Lord pointed out two things. MATTHEW 6:31-34— *So do not worry, saying, 'What shall we eat? or 'What shall we drink? or 'What shall we wear? For the pagans run after all these things, and your heavenly Father knows that you need them. But seek first his kingdom and his righteousness, and all these things will be given to you as well. Therefore do not worry about tomorrow, for tomorrow will worry about itself.*

First of all, our goal is not to run after these things but first seek the kingdom of God and then He will add all these things to our lives. It reminds me of another one of my favorite scriptures. PSALM 37:4— *Delight yourself in the Lord and He will give you the desires of your heart.* I used to like this verse because I wanted my "wish list" fulfilled. However, my focus was on the wrong part of the verse. It should have been on the first part of the verse, "Delight yourself in the Lord".

I realized that focusing on my desires was meaningless. My obsession to acquire material things shifted when I realized the happiness they brought never lasted. When that emotional high was over, I was again looking for the next thing to bring me happiness. Instead of fretting over my needs, I released them to the Lord and knew He would fulfill my desires in His timing.

MATTHEW 6:34—*"Do not worry about tomorrow..."* is also
an important factor. When I commit something to Him, it's
important that my heart stays in an active place of trust. Even
though I may not immediately see my prayer answered, I
continue to thank Him for it. I can rest knowing the Lord is
carefully watching over my requests.

MATTHEW 6:25-30— *Therefore I tell you, do not worry about
your life, what you will eat or drink; or about your body,
what you will wear. Is not life more important than food, and
the body more important than clothes? Look at the birds
of the air; they do not sow or reap or store away in barns,
and yet your heavenly Father feeds them. Are you not much
more valuable than they? Who of you by worrying can add a
single hour to his life? And why do you worry about clothes?
See how the lilies of the field grow. They do not labor or
spin. Yet I tell you that not even Solomon in all his splendor
was dressed like one of these. If that is how God clothes
the grass of the field, which is here today and tomorrow is
thrown into the fire, will he not much more clothe you, O you
of little faith?*

Just in case you haven't settled the issue of, "Do I have a right
to ask the Lord for something?" Let me point out what the scriptures say. MATTHEW 7:11— *So if you sinful people know how to
give good gifts to your children, how much more will your heavenly Father give good gifts to those who ask him.*[31] The scriptures
are full of verses that encourage us to ask Him for the things we
need. What's even more exciting is that the Lord *wants* to bless
us and shower us with good things from heaven.

This is a true story that perfectly explains my point. There was a
man who died and went to heaven, but came back and told what
he had experienced. When he arrived in heaven, he went for a
stroll with Jesus along a beautiful path. And as they walked and
talked, they came upon a huge warehouse. The door was standing ajar so he looked inside and saw it was completely filled with
wrapped packages. The man stopped and asked, "Jesus, what
are all those gifts?" Jesus replied, "That is your storehouse and

it is full of gifts for you." Bewildered by His response, he replied, "But Lord, I don't remember getting any of those packages while I was on earth." The Lord paused then gently responded, "Yes, I know. Many of them were delivered to you but because you didn't know how to receive them, they were returned to your warehouse."

When I heard this story, its reality jolted me. God has a warehouse of presents for each of us waiting to be delivered! I realized I had to change the way I responded to receiving gifts. My typical response was, "Oh, that is so nice of you but I couldn't possibly take it. I'm sure there is someone else who probably needs it more than I do. Thank you anyway." I suddenly realized if I wasn't able to receive from others, I probably wasn't receiving from the Lord either.

I had been living with a lop-sided belief system which made me think that "giving" was OK, but "receiving" was not. However, living under grace, we must be gracious givers *and* gracious receivers.

The new realization was difficult to embrace at first. I always felt guilty when I was given a special gift. Recognizing how wrong I had been, I told the Lord I was sorry for robbing Him and others of *their* blessing of giving. All of a sudden I felt a door in my heart was unlocked. The change took place when I repositioned my way of thinking. I became expectant of His blessings...not *demanding* but *expecting*.

His packages of blessings come in many different forms; deeper encounters with Him, friendships, ministry opportunities, health and healing, increased favor, a place to call home, financial blessings and yes, even as specific as a good hair day! I want to make it clear that my expectancy was not in *people* but the *Lord*. People will frequently disappoint us, that's why it's important to keep our eyes on the Lord to answer our prayers and petitions. He will never disappoint us. PSALM 118:8— *It is better to trust and take refuge in the Lord than to put confidence in man.*[32]

Now, each morning before I start my day, I pray, "Lord, don't return any gifts you are sending to me today. I gratefully receive them all. Amen."

Nuggets of Truth:

Some of you may be asking, "What was the significance of oil on the fence posts?" Carl and I firmly believe in anointing with oil. In this case, it was symbolic and a prophetic act of faith. In the Old Testament it was used to consecrate everyone and everything, or to declare an area of ground or a place as sacred and holy. EXODUS 40:9 AMP— *Take the anointing oil and anoint the tabernacle and everything in it; consecrate it and all its furnishings, and it will be holy.*

In the New Testament, anointing oil is used to anoint the sick and pray for them. JAMES 5:14— *Is any one of you sick? He should call the elders of the church to pray over him and anoint him with oil in the name of the Lord.* Samuel also anointed David with oil to set him apart for service to the Lord and commissioned him as God's representative. 1 SAMUEL 16:13— *So Samuel took the horn of oil and anointed him in the presence of his brothers, and from that day on the Spirit of the LORD came upon David in power.*

We dedicated our property and house to the Lord thereby declaring it off limits to the enemy. Even when we travel, there are times that I anoint the doorway and windows of our hotel room. It's the same principle; to declare it holy ground.

One last point to conclude, God moved on our behalf when Carl and I were finally united in our quest for a home. Until that point, I had been looking on my own. God stepped in and things moved faster when we both agreed it should happen. There is significant power in agreement. PSALM 133:1— *Behold, how good and pleasant it is when brothers dwell in unity! For there the LORD has commanded the blessing, even life forevermore.* When we finally agreed, the Lord "commanded" a blessing on our efforts. MATTHEW 18:19— *Again, I tell you that if two of you on earth agree about anything you ask for, it will be done for you by my Father in heaven.*

Meditation Questions

Take time to examine your heart and fill in the answers.

   1) Have you been chasing after material things? Make
       a list of them. What does it mean to you to seek His
       kingdom and His righteousness?

   _____

   _____

   _____

   _____

   2) What steps are you going to take to begin "delighting
       yourself in the Lord?"

   _____

   _____

   _____

   _____

   3) When you ask the Lord for certain things, do you try
       to guess what action He will take; therefore trying to
       "control" or "lead Him" to the response you want
       from Him? Is it hard for you to wait on His timing and
       an answer?

   _____

   _____

   _____

   _____

   4) Make a list of all the things you need from the Lord.
       Be specific concerning each request, then date it and
       trust Him with it as you release it to Him.

_____

_____

_____

_____

Prayer

As you read this prayer, make it your own.

> *Lord, I am sorry for not delighting in You the way I should. Instead, I have found delight in my self-made ambitions. Your word says that You know what I need even before I ask for it. Help me to focus on You, the Giver, not Your gifts. I am looking forward to finding greater joy in making You my first priority.*
>
> *I also need more grace to release my petitions after I have committed them to Your care. I want to close the door to worry and frustration and begin to walk in a place of increased faith even as I wait for these requests to be answered. Keep my heart steadfast and my eyes on You for only in You am I truly satisfied.*
>
> *I choose to trust You for all my needs and release the fulfillment of them to Your perfect care. Thank You for loving me so much. In Jesus' Name, Amen.*

Additional Scripture References

Take time to read these scriptures. They confirm that the Lord loves you and wants to answer your prayers. He wants to increase your faith and the power of your testimony.

MATTHEW 7:7— *Ask and it will be given to you; seek and you will find; knock and the door will be opened to you.*

MATTHEW 21:22— *If you believe, you will receive whatever you ask for in prayer.*

MATTHEW 6:8— *...for your Father knows what you need before you ask him.*

MARK 11:24— *Therefore I tell you, whatever you ask for in prayer, believe that you have received it, and it will be yours.*

JOHN 14:13-15— *And I will do whatever you ask in my name, so that the Son may bring glory to the Father. You may ask me for anything in my name, and I will do it.*

JOHN 16:24— *Until now you have not asked for anything in my name. Ask and you will receive, and your joy will be complete.*

Scripture to Memorize

PSALM 37:4— *Delight yourself in the Lord and He will give you the desires of your heart.*

Endnotes

[31]Scripture quotation taken from the Holy Bible, New Living Translation, copyright 1996, 2004. Used by permission of Tyndale House Publishers, Inc., Wheaton, Illinois 60189. All rights reserved.

[32]Scripture taken from the Amplified Bible, Copyright © 1954, 1958, 1962, 1964, 1965, 1987 by The Lockman Foundation. Used by permission

Chapter 10
CROSSING OVER

DAD'S DOCTOR WAS BLUNT AND CLEAR: "Jack, at this point, there's nothing more we can do for you. You might as well go home, you only have three to six months to live."

Dad had been ill for a while and, although his family had a history of cancer, he had put off going to see a doctor. Tests and exploratory surgery confirmed his dreaded suspicion. He had prostate cancer and his condition had already advanced beyond medical cure.

It felt like electricity raked through my body when I heard the news. I wanted to scream, "My father doesn't deserve this! He's been a faithful man who has ministered the gospel his entire life. How could this hideous disease issue a death sentence to yet another one of our family members?" The thought of losing my dad was unbearable. He was too young to "cross over"! We needed him here.

Dad, a true pioneer, never did anything in the conventional way. Chemotherapy and radiation were out of the question for him; he would fight the disease the all-natural way. So, Dad and Mom made radical changes in their eating habits. They searched through piles of books and the Internet for alternative cancer treatments. Most mornings, he made a "slurry," his word for the healthy green brew which looked like something you might find boiling out of a car radiator. He took the pitcher in one hand and tipped it to the ceiling, drinking the entire mixture.

Dinner in their home became a true adventure. We never knew what would be set before us. One thing for sure, it would be some new holistic recipe. We didn't mind trying new things. But, we sometimes declined a second helping.

Dad always believed that body, mind and spirit had to work together to bring complete health. He took his Bible and tabbed the scriptures that promised healing. He recited them everyday. His congregation, friends and family began fasting and praying for total healing. We all took an aggressive spiritual stance of battle against the enemy to contend for his healing.

When Dad walked into his doctor's office six months later, the doctor was shocked to see how well and full of life Dad was. In astonishment he said, "Jack, whatever you are doing, keep doing it!" Still not believing what he was seeing, he added, "I guess we need to run some more blood work and see what's going on." The results came back indicating Dad's cancer was gone! The news was riveting. We felt like the time bomb in Dad's body had just been defused. It was an absolute miracle; we won the battle!

Dad continued his healthy regime and life returned to normal. His healing bolstered everyone's faith. Life was good. But, six and a half years later my mother called with bad news: "Dad is not doing well again. The symptoms of cancer are back and his health is failing rapidly." Carl and I immediately made the eight-hour journey to be with Dad and Mom. When we arrived, Dad greeted us like he always did. But, this time he was more stooped and frail. His face was gaunt and his smile labored as we embraced in the doorway. Deep sadness gripped my heart. I knew these exchanges of affection were numbered.

I dearly loved my Dad. But I discovered a wall between us a few years earlier when my parents came to visit us. Dad and I jumped in the car to run some errands together. He liked to fix things at our house, so we dropped by Home Depot. When we returned, we sat in the driveway talking before going into the house. Feeling brave, I decided to ask him a question that had troubled me for a long time, "Dad, why don't you ever say you're proud of me?" His brow furrowed as he carefully and soberly stated, "Honey, you know I can't condone what you do for a living."

I thought he was joking. Surely he didn't mean that. After all,

I wasn't a hooker, drug dealer or exotic dancer; I was a worship leader and speaker. What about that could he not condone?

So, I asked, "You've got to be kidding me. Right?"

"Leann, the Scriptures are very clear about women. Their place is in the home with children, not in leadership." Still, I waited for a smile to emerge to let me know he was merely teasing. But by his lingering silence, I realized he was serious.

Finally it made sense. The friction and resistance I felt from him, every time I talked about my ministry travels, was because he thought I was walking in sin. The mystery was solved—doctrine and tradition had driven a wedge between us. Even though I knew he loved me, the very thing the Lord had called me to, and the passion that ran in my veins, was no longer open for conversation. I was crushed to think that a huge part of my life could no longer be shared with him.

I had never aspired to go into ministry. It was fine for my dad and others to be involved in ministry. But as a youth, ministry was not my passion. However, the Lord had other plans. As I grew older, He began to groom me for ministry and leadership. Since He called me, I had a choice to make. I could accept His call or I could reject it. I obeyed and accepted it.

Carl and I were certainly in agreement about my calling. In fact, he was one of my biggest cheerleaders. His respect and honor gave me the strength to walk through the doors of opportunity that the Lord opened.

In spite of the lack of support from my dad, I forged ahead. As an adult, I had to make decisions for myself. I would always be respectful to him, but ultimately I would answer to the Lord concerning His call on my life.

Many times I wanted to tell Dad about wonderful things and how God was moving in my life. But I couldn't. My heart ached to share my experiences with him. More than that, I wanted my earthly father's acceptance, affirmation and approval. Deeply disappointed,

I realized my heavenly Father would have to fill that void. In time, He did.

Thankfully, there were things Dad and I *could* share with each other. I could always spark his interest when I mentioned going fishing. Dad loved to fish! A plaque hung on his front porch read: "Born to fish, forced to work!" I had never had much luck fishing on the Mississippi River with him. After each trip, my throbbing welts and empty stringer were a dead give away I had gotten more mosquito bites than fish bites. But the fishing part didn't really matter that much to me; it was more about the "hang" than the catch anyway. I just liked to be with him.

As my father's health declined, I longed for one more fishing memory with him. So one cool but sunny October afternoon, I said, "Dad, maybe the fish will be biting today." He eventually expressed a frail, "Ok, let's give it a try." As I helped him to his feet, He took his time waiting for the strength to rise. Every movement took much more effort than it used to. I grabbed a tin can and we shuffled off to the best "worm dig" on the place. We turned over a few shovels of dirt and found lots of squishy worms under the shade of the big walnut trees. Shortly, Carl, Dad and I nestled into one of his "lucky" spots on a pond behind their house. In a matter of minutes, fishing poles, bobbers and sinkers were in full swing.

The late afternoon sun danced on the ripples of water like a field of diamonds. Every time a gentle breeze rustled the cattails, a new flurry of dragonflies and Indian summer silk filled the air. Leaves were falling and the fish were hungry. In less than an hour we had already caught 10 to 12 small perch. I had never caught so many fish! Dinner was going to be great; fried fish, dilled potato salad and an ice cold Pepsi.

Dad wanted to try one more favorite spot. Typically, he would scurry from one place to another along the bank to try his luck. But those days were over. Weakened by the disease and unsteady from the medications, he fished while resting in a lightweight plastic chair. As soon as he nestled into position, he cast his line.

It barely hit the water when he had a bite! Dad crouched forward, concentrating on just the right moment to pull and set the hook before he reeled it back in. He was so focused on the bobber that he didn't realize his weight had shifted. The front legs of the chair gave way in the muddy bank. In a split second he landed upside down, feet in the air, head and face buried in the shallow pond scum.

As I lifted him out of the water, he reeked of pond sludge. Sputtering and grunting through the mask of mud, I could see his big blue eyes twinkle and a smile emerge. He was shaken up but the morphine had cushioned the fall. He felt no pain. We collapsed onto the bank, exploding into hysterical laughter. With each peal of laughter, the years of disappointment and misunderstandings faded away like a river barge slipping away into a foggy night. Even though he lost that fish, our hearts found each other again that day. It was one of the best and last memories of our fishing days together.

One day, my brother Mark called. He had gone home for a visit and said the hospice nurse had just told them Dad's cancer had probably advanced to his brain. "It will only be a matter of days now."

Carl was away on business so I made the trip to my parents alone. As the miles passed, I tried to pray. Even listening to worship music didn't calm my panic. It was hard to believe my own father could be nearing the end of his life. When I arrived, Dad didn't greet me at the door as he always had before. Mom took me to his side, where he was resting quietly in a recliner. Slowly he opened his eyes and smiled, "Oh, it's Leann!"

Mom had cooked a delicious "comfort" meal that evening with everyone's favorite dishes; baked chicken, garlic mashed potatoes and gravy, fresh steamed broccoli, whole wheat rolls, and homemade coconut cream pie. The aroma and bountiful table setting made it almost like "old times." But, glancing over the kitchen counter into the living room, my father's pale silhouette brought me back to reality. I fought back the tears, already beginning to miss his presence in our family.

When dinner was ready Mark and I went into the living room to help Dad to the table. Mark asked, "Dad, would you like to come to the kitchen?" He replied, "Yes, but first I want to give my girl a hug." Mark carefully helped him up from his chair so we could embrace each other. Dad was famous for giving bear hugs, but not that day. He was a mere shadow of the strong man he used to be. We just held each other in a long and bittersweet embrace. That evening would be the last time his feet would shuffle to the dinner table.

Within that week, he declined rapidly and went from a wheel-chair to complete confinement in a hospital bed. When hospice delivered the bed we had to get rid of the sofa to make room for it. Dad tried to humor us, "Mary, I think it's time to burn that old couch. Besides, you needed to get a new one anyway." We wel-comed the levity and laughed while we joined the parade carrying the couch to the trash pile out back. Mark rolled Dad in his wheel chair through the snow so he could observe the torching of the couch. Soon, the roaring inferno pushed back the cold.

Over the next few days, we laughed and cried. We read the Bible to Dad, we prayed together, and we sang his favorite hymns. The increased dosage of morphine erased his inhibitions and he jum-bled simple words and sentences. *"Did you see that catfish float by on a log?" "Every time I close my eyes, I can't see."* One day after drinking his favorite beverage, buttermilk, he said, *"I'm fatisied"* instead of satisfied. He loved the laughter and joined in when he had the strength. The house was a buzz of activity. A constant flow of friends and family brought food and emotional support. We took turns giving him baths and swabbing out his mouth with liquid morphine, trying to bring comfort from the pain.

His bed was at the far side of the living room in the bay window where the couch used to be. Looking out at the bright reflecting snow, it reminded me that there *was* a world outside those four walls, one that *wasn't* dying. But I couldn't reach it. Standing at the end of the bed that afternoon, I felt helpless as I watched the sun, through leafless trees, cast shadows on his frail body.

One afternoon, Dad roused and sat up on the edge of the bed. Although he was groggy, his hands began to move in a circular motion, caressing one hand with the other while looking down as if he saw something in his lap. We asked, "Dad what are you seeing?" After a long pause he said, "I see angels."

"How many?"

"Lots of them" then repeated, "lots of them." With a faint smile lifting the corners of his mouth he continued, "I see Jesus too. He is here right now, holding my hand." Those words were like oxygen to me! Tears ran down my face. I could breathe easier just knowing he was already getting acquainted with the other side.

That evening Carl arrived. We all, including several visitors, joined hands and surrounded his bed for prayer. Dad grimaced as if he was wrestling with an unseen force. With Mom's permission, Carl leaned close to Dad's ear and spoke softly, "Dad, we will stand with you in whatever you and Jesus decide to do. If you want to be healed, we will continue to stand with you but if you want to go home, you are free to go. We will be fine with whatever you want to do. Don't worry about us; we will be all right. Be at peace." Then Carl anointed him with oil from head to toe and committed him to the Lord's care. Immediately, Dad grew quiet. The tension and redness in his face disappeared and he became still as if in a deep peaceful sleep.

It had grown late and the last visitor said goodbye. Exhausted, Carl and I retreated to our bedroom. He tried to comfort me, but no one could console my broken heart. I had never been so shaken by the cruelty of pain and suffering.

In the middle of the night, I got up to give Dad his medications. As I entered the living room, I could sense something was different. His breathing had become shallow. The gurgling sounds from his chest had grown louder and I saw that his legs and feet were beginning to "mottle." Under the skin, pools of blood were already marbling as his heart and circulation began to shut down. The hospice nurse had warned us that when we saw that condition, he would go quickly.

I called Mom and Carl. Mom said, "Do you think this is it?" I nodded and said, "Yes, I think we have come to the end." Just saying those words ushered both of us into a frenzied wail. I was crying so hard I could hardly breathe. He was slipping away and there was nothing we could do. Then, my knees went weak. Carl ran to me. He moved from one side of the bed to the other, trying to give support to Mom and me. Then his dry sense of humor broke the atmosphere, "It sure would make it a lot easier for me to hold you up if you two would stand on the *same* side of the bed!" But we couldn't help it. Both of us wanted to be as close to Dad's face as possible. All day, a CD had played soft and worshipful music in the room. At that moment, as if the orchestration of heaven came to earth, the artist sang:

The Lord bless you and keep you

The Lord make His face to shine upon you

And give you peace

And give you peace

The Lord lift His countenance upon you

The Lord bless you and keep you

The Lord make His face to shine upon you

And be gracious unto you

The Lord be gracious unto you[33]

As I heard those words, I cried out, "Please, Lord, I want to see beyond the natural realm. I want to see what's going on in heaven right now!" Suddenly, I saw Dad's silhouette walking on a beam of light entering magnificent jeweled gates. They were enormous and he looked so small in comparison. The light coming from within the gates was blinding but as I continued to look into the light, I saw heavenly beings filling the air. I couldn't see faces and I didn't see angel's wings. I saw outlines of a multitude of people. Then I heard them cheering and clapping. It was deafening. It sounded like a "war hero's" welcome home but he was the only one in the parade.

Then the Lord said to me, "He's home now." The vision had taken me by such surprise, I came out of it shouting, "Oh my gosh...Oh my gosh!" Mom yelled, "What …what is it?" I squealed, "I just saw Dad cross over!"

As I recounted what I had just seen for Mom and Carl, we felt a huge release. We were so relieved Dad didn't have to suffer anymore. The days of anguish and torment suddenly evaporated! The pain of his departure was replaced with the joy of his arrival. The sting of death was gone!

Within a matter of minutes Dad took one last breath then slowly released it. Pressing into his face, we saw big tears rolling from the corners of his eyes. I know they were tears of joy as he met Jesus, the One he loved, longed to be with and preached about his entire life.

We stood over him in complete silence. We had just seen my dad change worlds. Peace filled the room. It was a holy moment. On January 18, 2003 at 11:20 p.m. my father, Jack Hendrickson, finished his seventy-one year race on earth and received his reward. He stepped into eternal life with his best friend, Jesus.

Week Ten   [Date: _____]

Pick one day out of your week when you can take time to sit and reflect on the following thoughts and respond to the meditation questions below.

Content Point:

Tenth Key to Becoming Free: *Settle The Issue of Where You Will Spend Eternity.*

My father was ready for eternal life when he took his last breath. I was comforted to know he had already made his choice to live in heaven and I would see him again on the other side. However, you may not have made that decision yet, so I want to explain the importance of making it and help you understand what happens when you do.

In the normal course of things, every person will face death at some time in his life. However, there were only two men in history who did not see death in their lifetime; Enoch and Elijah. Genesis 5:23-24 says, *"He (Enoch) lived to be 365 years old. He walked with God then was no more because God took him away."* II Kings 2:11-12— *As they were walking along and talking together, suddenly a chariot of fire and horses of fire appeared and separated the two of them, and Elijah went up to heaven in a whirlwind. Elisha saw this and cried out, "My father! My father! The chariots and horsemen of Israel!" And Elisha saw him no more.*

Hebrews 9:27 says, *And just as each person is destined to die once and after that comes judgment.*[34] Since we do not know when our time on earth is finished, it is important to be ready to meet our Maker. Being sure of your eternal destiny is imperative. You have the choice of living eternity in heaven with God or in hell with Satan, separated from God. Heaven will be an endless existence of peace, love and happiness while hell will be one of torment, pain and loneliness…forever!

God has given every one a free will. He will not make that choice for you but is waiting and wants you to choose Him. He already died on the cross to take away your guilt and sin. The only thing you have to do is receive His free gift of salvation. You may not feel "worthy" of it or you may feel like you have to become a better person first or "get your act together" before you can make that decision. The truth is, no one is capable of being good enough to earn it. That's why it's *free*!

Since you can't save yourself, you need Jesus to save you. His gift of salvation is offered to any one who will receive it. John 3:16 says, *"For God so loved the world that He gave His one and only son so that every one who believes in Him will not perish but have eternal life."*

When you ask Him to forgive you, ask Him into your heart to also be Lord of your life. Every sin you have ever committed is immediately washed away, forgiven and forgotten. PSALM 103:12 says, *"As far as the east is from the west, so far has he removed our transgressions from us."* Salvation is like being able to push the "reset" button and start all over again. Truly, your spirit is born-again at that instant. It doesn't matter how many mistakes and failures you've made in your life, from that moment on, you receive a new beginning. The Lord will be with you to help and guide you. The Holy Spirit will come and make your heart His home. ACTS 2:38 says, *"Repent and be baptized, every one of you, in the name of Jesus Christ for the forgiveness of your sins. And you will receive the gift of the Holy Spirit."*

If you have never asked Jesus to come into your heart and to be Lord of your life, don't wait any longer. There is no guarantee how many days, months or years you have before you face eternity. Only the Lord knows your span of life. Today is the day to make that decision.

Again, there is nothing you can do to earn the gift of salvation. It is a gift from God; one He gives to all who ask for it. ROMANS 6:23— *For the wages of sin is death, but the gift of God is eternal life in Christ Jesus our Lord.* Ask Him for it. He is waiting.

Allow the Lord to come into your life as you read along with the prayer at the end of this chapter.

Nuggets of Truth:

There are times when we lose loved ones who have not clearly chosen to believe. Of course, our first response is to mourn the fact that we may never see them again. However, I would like to offer some hope.

We do not truly know the heart of a man. Only God does. He is also the only One who will judge us when our life is over. Since I am not God, I don't know when someone's "last chance" is given. No one really knows what happens in the final moments between this life and eternity. I do know, however, we are not to bear the burden of judgment. That is God's responsibility. 1 SAMUEL 16:7 says, *The Lord said to Samuel, "The Lord does not look at the things man looks at. Man looks at the outward appearance, but the Lord looks at the heart."*

It also says in 2 PETER 3:9— *He is long-suffering toward you, not desiring that any should perish, but that all should turn to repentance.*[35] Clearly, we must choose to trust the Lord to show mercy. Then we have to release them to Him and let them go. Ask the Lord for comfort, strength and the grace to do that.

Grieving the loss of a loved one is all part of life. Grieving is natural and necessary. Everyone will experience it at some point but it is important to allow the Lord to take your grief so you don't also "die" with the one who has passed. The Lord does not desire that you continue living in a state of grief. He wants to heal your heart. PSALM 147:3 says, *"He heals the brokenhearted and binds up their wounds."* Also, ISAIAH 51:12 says, *"I, even I, am He who comforts you."* You are still alive and God has incredible plans for you. You don't have to give up on life. As time passes, allow His love to wash away the pain of loss, and restore your joy. He will give you a reason to smile and laugh again.

Meditation Questions

Take time to examine your heart and fill in the answers.

1) What are your thoughts on "crossing over" to eternity?

_____

_____

_____

_____

2) What do you expect Heaven to be and look like? Do you expect to see God and Jesus?

_____

_____

_____

_____

3) Do you believe God wants to accept you and forgive you for what you've done in your life?

_____

_____

_____

_____

4) Have you ever asked Jesus to come into your heart and be Lord of your life? If you have not, are you ready to do so now? If you already have, describe what that experience was like.

_____

_____

_____

_____

5) In light of your decision, make sure you tell someone; your pastor, priest, spouse or friend about your new commitment to Jesus. Complete this step by noting the date and the person's name.

_____

_____

_____

_____

Prayer

As you read this prayer, make it your own.

> *Jesus, I confess that I am a sinner. I believe You are the Son of God and that You died on the cross to save me. I believe You are the only Way, the Truth and the Life. Please forgive me for all my sins. Jesus, I invite You into my heart. Make it Your home. I want You to be Lord and Savior of my life. And, Jesus, I want to live fully committed to You, to grow into maturity as Your child. I thank You that my name is now written in the Lamb's Book of Life and I will spend eternity with You. Also, baptize me with the Holy Spirit who empowers me to live in covenant with You. Thank You. In Jesus' Name, Amen.*

Additional Scripture References

Take time to read these scriptures. They confirm who Jesus is, why He came to earth, the importance of salvation, and what the scripture says about death.

JOHN 14:6— *Jesus answered, "I am the Way and the Truth and the Life. No one comes to the Father except through me."*

TITUS 2:11— *For the grace of God that brings salvation has appeared to all men.*

1 JOHN 1:9— *If we confess our sins, he is faithful and just and will forgive us our sins and purify us from all unrighteousness.*

1 THESSALONIANS 5:9— *For God did not appoint us to suffer wrath but to receive salvation through our Lord Jesus Christ.*

EPHESIANS 1:13— *And you also were included in Christ when you heard the word of truth, the gospel of your salvation. Having believed, you were marked in him with a seal, the promised Holy Spirit.*

JOHN 3:3— *In reply Jesus declared, "I tell you the truth, no one can see the kingdom of God unless he is born again."*

1 THESSALONIANS 4:13-14— *Brothers, we do not want you to be ignorant about those who fall asleep, or to grieve like the rest of men, who have not hope. We believe that Jesus died and rose again and so we believe that God will bring with Jesus those who have fallen asleep in Him.*

PSALM 116:15— *Precious in the sight of the Lord is the death of His saints.*

ROMANS 8:38— *For I am convinced that neither death nor life, neither angels nor demons, neither the present nor the future, nor any powers, neither height nor depth, or anything else in all creation, will be able to separate us from the love of God that is in Christ Jesus our Lord.*

Scripture to Memorize

JOHN 3:16— *For God so loved the world that he gave his one and only Son, that whoever believes in him shall not perish but have eternal life.*

Endnotes

[33]Artist: Gary Pigg / www.garypigg.com. Title: "The Blessing" - from the project "Like Him" Words: Numbers 6:24-26. Music by Gary Pigg

[34]Scripture quotation taken from the Holy Bible, New Living Translation, copyright 1996, 2004. Used by permission of Tyndale House Publishers, Inc., Wheaton, Illinois 60189. All rights reserved.

[35]Scripture taken from the Amplified Bible, Copyright © 1954, 1958, 1962, 1964, 1965, 1987 by The Lockman Foundation. Used by permission

Chapter 11

THE GREAT EXCHANGE

THE WHOLE WORSHIP TEAM SPILLED OUT OF THE VAN in Wichita, Kansas and made a beeline for the church platform. We had to get the sound check underway. The instruments, microphones and monitors needed to be tweaked and all the songs had to be rehearsed before that evening's worship event. It went so smoothly we finished early.

Since I had extra time, I went to the lobby to help my friend Karen set up the product table. We emptied box after box of books and CDs, but the stack of unpacked merchandise didn't seem to be getting any smaller. I had just commented on how overwhelmed I was at the many books that had been written and said, "Who has time to read all these books?" Karen and I were so absorbed in our conversation that I did not see a man pick up one of them from the table. At a break in our conversation, he said, "Now here's a book you really *need* to read." Startled, I spun around to see who had spoken. A man I did not know held a book out to me and said, "This book will make a *godly* woman out of you." I was instantly annoyed that a stranger had taken the liberty to interrupt our conversation. Not only was he rude, but he was also blatantly personal.

Suddenly I felt like I had been slapped in the face as his words began to sink in. *Maybe this guy is a prophet and had seen some glaring "wickedness" in my life. But if he was a prophetic messenger, he certainly had no gift of love by which to deliver it. He had no right to pronounce such flippant judgment that implied I wasn't a godly woman! After all, I was one of the singers and clinicians for a well-known worship band at the conference.*

I tried to just dismiss him as a jerk. But, his words struck deep.

Looking away from his gaze, I struggled to regain my composure.

Battling the impact of his words, I ran to the nearest ladies room. Making my way through the smell of restroom deodorizer, I locked myself in the closest stall. I prayed, I confessed, I tried all the spiritual steps I knew to forgive this guy and stop the echo of his implied insult. It didn't work; the more I prayed, the madder I got. I couldn't find God anywhere! Where did He go?

I desperately tried to pull myself together while patting my tears and reapplying lip gloss. In a very short time I had to walk out on stage and lead people into the Presence of God. I didn't want anyone else to see the dagger lodged in my heart.

As I walked onto the stage, I hoped to find His Presence and recover from what had just happened. But, sitting there on the front row, right in front of me, was "The Jerk." Even though everyone else seemed to be swept into worship, I was not. I was like a kite reaching for the wind. Each note searched for the lift of the Spirit, but only found a downdraft from my heavy heart. I thought the night would never end! About an hour later, I was relieved when we paused to take an offering.

After the offering, the emcee made an extravagant introduction of the evening speaker. He sounded so wonderful I couldn't wait to hear him speak. And, then "The Jerk" stood and walked to the podium! I felt nauseous. I couldn't tell you a thing he said because I was fuming on the inside. The scene with Charlie Brown's schoolteacher came to mind. All I heard was, "Whah… whah..whah…whah..whah…whah...whah..." After an exhausting hour, he finally wrapped it up.

Of course, I was well aware of what the Bible says about forgiveness. COLOSSIANS 3:13— *Bear with each other and forgive whatever grievances you may have against one another. Forgive as the Lord forgave you.* But I wasn't there. So, how could I minister the love of the Lord to others while I was wrestling with my own anger and unforgiveness? I tried to stuff my crisis into a mental lockbox but it seeped out and affected everything I did. I had no "flow" to teach or sing the entire weekend. My life was out of cadence. Every conversation seemed awkward and forced.

By the time we flew home on Sunday, my injured heart was inflamed. My whole body felt sick. And my wound had grown into an infectious resentment. I wanted to be alone! I was mad at the whole world. Monday morning, I could hardly raise my head. A shroud of depression loomed over me; I knew I had to get help. I felt like death.

As the morning sun grew brighter, so did my courage. I headed for the track with Winston and Clementine, our two chocolate Labradors. I needed a good run and so did they. The harder I ran, the "hotter" I got as the "The Jerk's" words screamed in my head. Rivers of sweat and tears zigzagged down my face. Torrents of anger and bitterness exploded in all its ugliness.

As I ran, the floodwaters of my soul began to recede. I asked the Lord, "Why have the words of that man gripped my heart like this?" Then I clearly heard the gentle voice of the Lord, "You are shaken because he challenged your identity. The very essence of your life has been brought into question by the implication of one single statement."

Slowing my pace, He continued to speak to me. He asked, "Who are you going to believe? The opinion of a *person* or *My* opinion of you?" All of a sudden the scales fell off of my eyes and there before me was a doorway of hope. The simple truth was that I didn't have to accept any other voice. I had received a guilty judgment from someone I didn't even know. I had let myself be imprisoned in…a lie.

While finishing the final lap, the Lord affirmed His love for me and reminded me of who I was. He brought to mind all the scriptures that confirmed His affection toward me.

You are a delight to me and you are the apple of my eye.
—Deuteronomy 30:9 and Psalm 17:8

He brought me out into a spacious place; he rescued me because he delighted in me. —2 SAMUEL 22:20

I chose you before the creation of the world; to be holy, set apart and without fault in My sight; to be above reproach before Me in love. —EPHESIANS 1:4

My love is complete in you. —I JOHN 4:12

I give you lots of grace to grow—PROVERBS 1:9

I hand picked you and carved you in My image.—GENESIS 1: 27

I am pleased to see My likeness in you.—ROMANS 8:29

He lavished His love on me. With each step, my heart got lighter. I recited His words over and over again, allowing them to annihilate the chains of accusation and hopelessness that held me just moments before. His healing oil of truth and acceptance sank to the deepest crevasses of my heart. I could feel transformation taking place.

He showed me I was preoccupied with what other people thought of me. I had made idols of them and their opinions. I looked for their affirmation to define my worth instead of finding it in Him.

An hour later, when I had finished running, I returned home a new woman. There was no trace of pain in my heart. The Lord had silenced the echoes of the accuser and restored my true identity.

The next morning my phone rang. An unfamiliar voice said, "Hello Leann." After an awkward silence he continued, "This is George." It was the "jerk"! I nearly dropped the phone. Since we had never officially met at the conference, I was shocked he would contact me.

In my most "professional" voice, I replied, "Oh… hi, George."

"Leann, I understand I said something this weekend that was very hurtful to you."

It took me a few seconds to respond. "Well…Yes, you did."

"I am so sorry I offended you. What did I say?" I could tell he genuinely had no idea what he had said.

As I replayed the scenario at the product table, he interrupted, "Oh no, no! That's not what I meant at all! My excitement was simply because I had just finished reading that book. It so impacted me that it changed *my life*! My enthusiasm for the book was because of what it did for me! That came across completely wrong. I am so sorry! Would you please forgive me?"

I chuckled. It was hard to believe how Satan had distorted our brief interaction a few days ago.

"George, I have already forgiven you. Actually, when I got home, I was able to get alone with the Lord and He helped me let go of the sting of what I *thought* you meant."

As I hung up the phone, I knew my heart was completely clear.

No more screams. Inside or out. No turmoil. The Lord had healed me completely.

Over the years, I've learned that God's truth is "reality." When we find ourselves "screaming on the inside," it is because we've embraced a lie. And when we believe a lie, we empower the liar who is Satan.

Unknowingly, we fall into his plan to destroy our lives.

But that does not need to be the end of the story. Just run to the One Who created you, sustains you, and loves you. You can always be real with Him.

Jesus said, *"The words I have spoken to you are spirit and they are life."* —JOHN 6:63. His words are sweet, everlasting, and power-ful. They can turn your heart into a peaceful sanctuary.

The Creator-God of the universe wants to make you completely whole and well again. He will make your insides a scream-free zone.

Week Eleven   [Date: _____]

Pick one day out of your week when you can take time to sit and reflect on the following thoughts and respond to the meditation questions below.

Eleventh Step to Becoming Free: *Replace the Lie with Truth.*

Sometimes, forgivness comes easier than other times. You know those times…when you are slammed with an insult or a "hot button" is pushed. I used to think it was a simple act of mind over matter. If I could quote enough scriptures, say, *"I forgive you"* enough times, somehow I could psych myself out of the trauma of it. As I look back, in most cases, it never really worked. The pain was merely covered up with the busyness of life for a while and time helped to lessen its sting.

The Holy Spirit has taught me that forgiveness is not an exercise of the mind, but is a supernatural transaction of the heart. We are crippled by an offense at a vulnerable point when Satan screams a lie. Subconsciously, we receive that lie and try to adopt it as truth but it doesn't fit. It doesn't fit because it doesn't line up with who and what the Word of God says we are. The pain comes when we try to incorporate that lie into our belief system. When we are not secure in *who* we are and filled with the truth of the Word, it leaves the door wide open for Satan to make us believe something false.

This is how it works. Many times a lie is blatantly stated or implied by someone in word or action. Satan's job is to convince us of anything that will betray our confidence in the Lord and in ourselves. If the lie is not recognized at the onset, its deceit germinates into a blockage that keeps us from seeing the truth of *who* the Lord says we are. Words like… "You'll never be good enough, you're worthless, you're not capable of doing things right, you're not worthy of God's love, you're too fat…. or too thin, too young …or too old, you're ugly, unloved and unwanted, rejected or you just don't fit in anywhere, or.....God allowed something bad to happen to me therefore He doesn't love me, or I don't deserve to be loved." Do any of these lies sound familiar? They are nothing more than a web of deception to belittle you and make you want to give up.

That delineation of truth becomes clearer when we are born again. When we invite Jesus to come in and live in our heart, He becomes our plumb line of truth. His Spirit in us knows what is true and what is not. The more we study the Word and the more we spend time with the Lord, that truth becomes clearer.

The same is true when you get a speck of dust or an eyelash in your eye. Our eye knows the foreign object is not supposed to be there and will continue to pulsate with pain until the foreign body is removed. As it is taken out, the pain leaves.

The Lord always speaks the truth to us and if we will take the time to listen, He is speaking right now. He will always use His Word to confirm the truth. It is easy to tell whether it is God or Satan speaking to us by whether it lines up with the Word of God. If it lines up with scripture, our heart will know it and it will feel like a comforting blanket of peace.

It's important to realize the Lord *wants* us to walk in complete freedom from our past. He is patient and desires to meet with us for "heart surgery" as many times as we need Him to. However, we have to go after our rightful inheritance of freedom from the lies of yesterday. Every time a lie is broken, Satan loses more control over us. Each time a lie is replaced with the Truth, another "hot button" is diffused so that Satan or people can no longer push it.

When you have finished walking through the steps at the end of this chapter, you will find a new freedom. However, that freedom may be tested but don't be afraid. All you need to do is declare the truth again out loud......just like I did when the Lord spoke to me on the track. I recited it over and over again until it sank deep into my spirit. Do it as many times as the old lie is thrown into your face. Trust me, pretty soon Satan will give up because he knows you are staking claim to the truth and you are not letting go of it.

Always remember, just as reciting a lie over and over again brings pain and death to your soul, reciting His truth over and over again brings life. If you need Him to remind you of His love and promises, just ask Him. He delights in speaking them to you as many times as you need to hear them.

Nuggets of Truth

Satan wants to destroy us and one of his tricks is to distort our interpretation or understanding of a situation. He will do anything possible to bring a wedge or division between two people. For instance in my own marriage, there are times I'll turn and look at Carl with a bewildered expression, knowing he didn't hear what I just said by how he responded to it. What I said seemed quite clear to me, however, as he listened, he heard my words through his own "filters." His filters are unique to him, formed by his own experience and knowledge. There are times when the tone in my voice speaks louder than what I actually said. We've learned to stop and clarify what we meant before proceeding with the conversation. It reminds us of the Abbot & Costello routine, "Who's On First." When we hit those moments, we burst into laughter and say, "Maybe we should just start over so we can both get on the same "page".

This can happen with friendships and casual acquaintances as well. When a comment feels like a "sting" as it enters your mind, it's OK to stop and politely ask, "Would you please clarify what you said so I don't misunderstand you?" An offense grows with time. It's better to address a possible offense when it happens rather than having to embrace the painful and arduous task of working through it later.

That's probably what I should have done when George made his comment. However, I was too intimated and shocked to respond to it. So instead of questioning him, I drew my own conclusion and allowed Satan to disable me for the next few days.

When you are offended, you become an "offense magnet." Everything offends you. However, when your heart is clear, it's hard to get offended. Even if someone is being rude, his or her jab has no belief system by which to be attached because your heart is free.

It's important *not* to base your release from an offense contingent on an apology from the person who offended you. Whether it is a spouse, friend or relative, you can't wait for it. If you do, you may linger in a wounded state for the rest of your life…and life's too short for that! You can't change someone else. The only person you are responsible for and have control over is YOU. I have learned I *can* forgive another person without their apology. I have proven it over and over and it has worked every time. When this reality finally hit me, I stopped waiting for an apology. I took responsibility for the condition of my own heart. When I went after my own freedom, I found it.

To further illustrate my point, this scenario has occasionally happened in our twenty-six years of marriage. There have been times when Carl and I have had an argument, and he came to apologize. I refused. In my self-centered state, I wanted to stay mad a little longer, so I did. In fact, I stayed miserable until I was good and tired of it and ready to let it go.

So you see, when Carl asked me to forgive him, I had a choice to make. Just his asking me didn't change the hurt in my heart. It took my deliberate action of wanting to let the offense go before the transaction could be completed. Becoming free was strictly a matter between the Lord and me. No one else could make it complete.

When I am full of the Spirit, I have the strength to choose not to be offended. Even if the insult is blatantly unfair, I have a choice to make. PROVERBS **12:16**— *A fool shows his annoyance at once, but a prudent man overlooks an insult.* In difficult situations, I even say it out loud to myself…"I will not be offended." Before long Satan leaves.

There's an easy way to know whether an offence is "alive" or "dead" in our hearts. When the hurtful scenario is replayed in your memory, "If it hurts, it ain't dead yet." Don't stop going after the truth and replacing all the lies until the pain is gone.

Prayer

As you read this prayer, make it your own.

> *Lord Jesus, You are the Great Physician. My heart has been wounded by other's words or actions and I need Your help. You can see every detail of my past and all the times Satan had access to my heart. He tried to make me believe something that wasn't true. Words and wrong beliefs have kept me in a prison and left me crippled— spiritually, mentally and emotionally. Today, I want to be free of the pain of those paralyzing lies. I want to be whole again and completely healed by Your truth.*
>
> *Jesus, would you walk with me through these following steps to bring full release from every lie I believed. I want to let go of every thought or mind set that does not line up with Your Word. Speak to me and show me Your Truth.*
>
> *Thank You, Jesus, for changing my life and setting me free. I love You. Amen.*

Meditation Questions

Give yourself plenty of time to complete the following questions, exercises and prayer. If you are uncomfortable in doing the following workbook section alone, you may want to ask a trusted believing Christian to help you walk through these steps.

1) Have you ever experienced pain from something negative that was implied about you or spoken directly to you? If yes, write down what happened. If your answer is no, ask Jesus to remind you of any moments you may have forgotten. The point is to uncover all offenses and be free from them.

_____

_____

_____

_____

.

2) What distortions or lies did you "believe" that
   brought the pain? Examples: "I am not loved," "I am
   not wanted", "No one values me," "I'm not good
   enough," "I'm not smart enough," "I'm not pretty
   enough or young enough," etc. There may be more
   than one thing, so wait and listen as Jesus reveals it to
   you then write it down.

_____

_____

_____

_____

3) Now, ask Jesus to take you back to the place where
   that belief or lie originated. That painful place may
   have happened for the first time recently or Satan
   may have planted that seed of pain when you were a
   child. Wait for Jesus to show you where Satan first had
   access into your life with that lie. It may help to close
   your eyes. Many times the Lord brings back memories
   in a visual picture through your "mind's eye".

_____

_____

_____

_____

4) Ask Jesus to speak His truth to you now. Even though you weren't aware the Lord was there during your time of crisis, He was, and He is also with you now. Hebrews 13:5— ... *because God has said, "Never will I leave you; never will I forsake you."* He is standing in the middle of your crisis, waiting to redeem that moment in your life. Wait for Him to speak to you then write down what He said. Examples: "I love you," "You are forgiven, and it wasn't your fault." "You are beautiful just the way I made you," "I want your friendship," "You are special and precious to Me."

Complete this step by adding the date and time to your notes.

_____

_____

_____

_____

5) Is the pain gone? As you remember the distorted lie that brought the pain, how does your heart feel? As you meditate on the truth and let it sink into your heart, the lie will be broken and the pain will be gone. The great exchange will have been made. His truth is far more powerful than any lie of Satan! John 8:32— *Then you will know the truth and the truth will set you free.*

_____

_____

_____

_____

6) An important last step is to release the offender into Jesus' care. Put their hand in the hand of Jesus and let them go. Using his/her name, declare out loud that you forgive them and release them.

_____

_____

_____

_____

Repeat these steps as many times as is necessary because our hurtful past may resemble an onionskin. Some of you will have layers of pain to work through. I did. So keep meeting with the Lord and let Him bring Truth to every place that needs healing. Don't give up. He wants you to be free of pain and full of love, joy and hope. It's your time to be scream-free!

Additional Scripture References

Take time to read these scriptures. They will strengthen you as you are reminded of His promises to you.

MATTHEW 18:21-22— *Then Peter came to Jesus and asked, "Lord, how many times shall I forgive my brother when he sins against me? Up to seven times?" Jesus answered, "I tell you, not seven times, but seventy times seven times.*

LUKE 6:37— *Do not judge, and you will not be judged. Do not condemn, and you will not be condemned. Forgive, and you will be forgiven.*

ROMANS 8:33-34—*Who dares accuse us whom God has chosen for his own? No one—for God himself has given us right standing with himself. Who then will condemn us? No one— for Christ Jesus died for us and was raised to life for us, and he is sitting in the place of honor at God's right hand, pleading for us.*

ROMANS 8:1—*Therefore, there is now no condemnation for those who are in Christ Jesus.*

Scripture to Memorize

PROVERBS 19:11— *A man's wisdom gives him patience; it is to his glory to overlook an offense.*